5
QUESTIONS
OF THE
INQUISITIVE
APES

5
QUESTIONS
OF THE
INQUISITIVE
APES

Contemporary Answers to Ancient Questions

SUBHRASHIS ADHIKARI

Srishti
PUBLISHERS & DISTRIBUTORS

SRISHTI PUBLISHERS & DISTRIBUTORS
Registered Office: N-16, C.R. Park
New Delhi – 110 019
Corporate Office: 212A, Peacock Lane
Shahpur Jat, New Delhi – 110 049

editorial@srishtipublishers.com

First published by
Srishti Publishers & Distributors in 2019

10 9 8 7 6 5 4 3 2 1

Printed at Repro Knowledgecast Limited, Thane

To all story weavers.

Contents

Acknowledgements

5Questions of the Inquisitive Apes is my second book after *The Journey of Survivors – 70,000-Year History of Indian Subcontinent.* My journey of writing started with my blog Khoj. The idea to publish first came to my mind when I started to get few requests to publish the blog articles from my blog readers. I would like to thank them for considering my writing worth publishing and inspiring me to write. Reading books and scientific articles, interacting, conversing, debating and sometimes even fighting with people gave me strange ideas and shocking revelations. In that process, I made friends with enemies, and enemies of friends. Special thanks to authors like Vivekananda, Bryson B., Dawkins R., Diamond J., Harari Y.N., Hawking S., Mukherjee S., and countless others for turning me into an inquisitive ape. This book is a result of that, and I would like to take this opportunity to thank all those friends and 'enemies' who contributed to my thoughts.

I would like to thank my parents for making me who I am. Special thanks to my brother for introducing me to the world of books. Thanking my wife for her patience and constant support would not be enough. Her friends call her Zen (derived from Sanskrit word *dhyana*, or 'meditative state'). Her amazingly unbiased mind has silently influenced my thoughts over the years. My daughter has helped me evolve as a father, and as a person. I would like to thank my entire family for their constant encouragement.

Thanks to everyone on the Srishti Publishers team who helped me so much. I would like to express gratitude to Arup Bose, my publisher for his support. To Stuti for doing an excellent job on the manuscript and for her patience in correcting my horrible grammar.

Last but not the least, I would like to beg forgiveness to those who have stood by me for years, and whose names I have failed to mention.

Preface

'The important thing is not to stop questioning; curiosity has its own reason for existing. One cannot help but be in awe when contemplating the mysteries of eternity, of life, of the marvelous structure of reality. It is enough if one tries merely to comprehend a little of the mystery every day. The important thing is not to stop questioning; never lose a holy curiosity.'

— Albert Einstein, statement to William Miller, as quoted in *Life* magazine (2 May 1955)

How often has it happened that you met an idiot who turned your usual bad day into a perfect horror? It was a rainy morning, not quite the day I was looking forward to. I had to catch the morning Shatabdi to Bhopal and the unusual rain made the Delhi roads choke, as usual. Being used to the traffic in the capital of India, I started two hours early. Which also meant that I did not get my full quota of sleep. Thank goodness I did so. My seasoned driver drove through the murky roads, maneuvering through the swarm of cars to reach just on time. Right after I boarded the train, even before I could reach my seat, the train started. Things here happen on time whenever you least want them to. Half awake and half wet, I trotted through the narrow compartment to reach my window seat, only to find it occupied by a young man. The young man, in his mid-twenties, looked at me bluntly, happy to steal my seat, and with it, my view. After a failed attempt at logic with him and his father, I resigned to my fate and chose peace in the aisle seat.

I sat there, absorbed in my own blue funk, when my gaze fell upon my seat-thief. As if sitting on my allotted seat was not enough, it seemed like the guy derived some sort of pervert pleasure by getting on my nerves. He kept staring at me, smiling, without uttering a single word. When the food was served, he stared at his food, and then mine, in a way as if he was seeing food for the first time. Everything seemed to make him happier than it would a normal person. His smile was so out of sync with my awful day that my jealousy about his happiness seemed to make me even angrier. As the rain stopped and the sun shone through the broken clouds, the view of the outside became clearer. The guy on my seat said to his father, 'Look, Dad! The trees are moving backwards!' That was when I realized there was something wrong with him. I quietly asked his dad if everything was all right. The dad's reply shocked me. It was not the answer I was expecting. His words made me feel bad, not about him, but about myself. There was nothing wrong with him. If at all, there was something wrong with me. My seat thief was not a mentally unstable person, but a perfectly normal young man. Until just a few days back, he was blind. He was returning home today after a successful eye operation. It was indeed the first time he could relate to all that he felt throughout his life with his new-found visual pleasure. Who can blame him for taking my damn seat!

As you might have guessed by now, this is a story. Our brain is wired to comprehend stories better than facts or stats. As you read this book, you will get to know why. When our narratives do not match that of others, we have a conflict. How often have we failed to look at the world through the perspective of someone else? How often have we blamed others for our bad day? How often have we missed the truth, blinded by our prejudice? In an argument when one thinks that the opponent is completely wrong, he automatically assumes that he himself is absolutely right. He assumes that he knows everything about the topic of the argument, and there is nothing more that he needs to know. Needless to say, such egoistic judgments are often wrong. When we keep arguing, thinking that the other person is not getting our point of view, we often ignore the fact that we are not getting theirs either. There is always more to learn. There is always another side of the coin. There can always be more than one truth. The want to know more is what prevents science from becoming scientism or religion. It is okay to be wrong once in a while.

Human beings have strong memories. These memories help us make sense of the world around us. To understand something new, we fall back on our old memories, try to correlate with known things and come to an inference about the new thing. It can be said with fair certainty that our past memories determine the way in which we react to situations. And most often than not, our reaction determines our future. In order to have the right future, it is important that we have the right memories. And, more importantly, look at memories in a right way. The right way is the way of questioning, understanding and keeping one's mind open. A bit of scepticism is always healthy. It is an evolutionary tool that has kept us alive for millions of years, and the good news is that we are instinctively quite good at questioning.

You must have often heard that we have evolved from apes. Let me convey to you that it is a lie. We have not evolved from apes, we *are* apes! We are the fifth species of great apes, along with chimpanzees, bonobos, gorillas and orangutans. The only possible difference between us and other animals is that we ask too many questions, even in times of emergency. When a deer gives a signal of danger, the entire herd runs without questioning the judgment of the one who gave the warning. Compare that to what humans do. When the fire alarm in our office starts to ring, the first action should be to evacuate. Instead, the first thing that comes to our mind is always the question 'What is it?' Is it a fire, an earthquake, a planned drill or just a false alarm? Our brain is hard wired to ask questions. These questions helped our ancestors in mitigating the dangers appropriately. In this book I will make an attempt to make sense of five big questions. These questions have been bothering me for quite some time. This book is a collection of whatever sense I could make about these questions from the little knowledge I have gained from the latest researches in various fields of science. Many people have tried to answer these questions before, and my attempt is not a new one. Often such difficult questions have been explained as acts of god. People have even tried to justify the existence of the creator from the shape of a banana! To me, such explanations are nothing but running away from taking the difficult path of finding the right answers. Even if you believe in god, make an attempt to answer the hows and whats. That way your faith would be more satisfying.

The first question is, 'How we came to be?' Was it by design, chance, or as anthropic principle would suggest, we just are because had the universe been any different, there would have been no us to ask the question? Once we know how we came to be the next logical question would be to understand how we make sense our universe. In this chapter, we would know how our sense organs are acquiring information and then processing and interpreting the reality with biases and heuristics implanted in our brain. We will see how breakthroughs in quantum physics are breaking the fortress of reality we have built around us. The same fortress creates morality, bigotry, and taboos. That would bring us to the question, 'Is sex bad?' Once we manage to crumble down the fortress, we are ready to take on the profound question 'Who are we?' Is there really a unique 'us'? The final question is the one that human beings are seeking since the very beginning, 'How to be happy?' Can our external world make us happy, or is happiness just the biochemistry of our brain? Research on happiness is slowly shifting from the domain of philosophy and psychology to that of biology. Is the modern understanding of the question any different from those of the ancient philosophers? Can the contemporary knowledge guide us to a happy life?

One needs to be very careful here and appreciate that science does not have answers to all the questions. And many of the answers are theories. Established scientific theories have been repeatedly tested and have withstood rigorous scrutiny of time. They are pretty solid. However, theories no matter how good, are hypothetical and might turn out to be false. Scientific observations are empirical and if the results can be reproduced over and over again, it becomes a law. The interpretation of such results has their own uncertainties. Then there are testable explanations and hypothesis, which has a lot of uncertainty. The aim of this book is not to provide one single answer to all the questions, but generate more questions in the mind of the reader. If this book manages to increase the inquisitiveness of the readers, I will consider my attempt a success.

Question 1

How We Came To Be?

☙❧

'By the most astounding stroke of luck an infinitesimal portion of all the matter in the universe came together to create you and for the tiniest moment in the great span of eternity you have the incomparable privilege to exist.'

– Bill Bryson, *I'm a Stranger Here Myself: Notes on Returning to America after Twenty Years Away* (1999)

Looking for a place to rest

One of the most thrilling experiences of my life happened in one of the holiest places of India, Chitrakoot. Legend has it that King Rama, his wife Sita, and brother Lakshmana spent eleven out of their fourteen years of exile here. My group and I were also there for a fourteen-day exile, looking at the rock outcrops of Vindhyan. After our usual long day walk, I stumbled upon a rock formation named the Tirohan Dolomite. There I was, staring down at one of the oldest evidences of life preserved in the rocks. What I was looking at were our fossilized tiny ancestors – the phosphatized stromatolitic microbialites. These stromatolites are a variety of red algae that lived 1.6 billion years ago. They are one of the oldest direct evidences of life. Isn't that fascinating? What's more fascinating is to try and trace back the evolution of the thinking, gossiping, inquisitive apes from those humble creatures.

All ancient societies have stories of how we came to be. According to one myth of the Bantu tribe of Africa, God Bumba vomited life and the universe. We all are a product of the giant pale-skinned Bumba's vomit. Don't ask me what he consumed before spewing. The Egyptian myth is going to make even the Bantu tribe's story sound decent. As written in the *Hymn to Atum*, there was nothing before Atum, the one who willed himself into being. Don't know why, maybe he was bored, so he started to self-stimulate. The bizarre part is that he ejaculated into his own mouth, and then he spat out the semen that resulted in a spunk rain. Everything else was created from that rain. Luckily, not all origin stories are so gross, but most of them start with chaos. So does the Greek story. From chaos filled with darkness came the primordial goddess Gaia – the earth and the mother of all life. From her was born the starry sky, Uranus, who wrapped around her like an eternal lover. Together, the sky and the earth produced many children – good, bad and ugly. From hideous and malformed Hecantonchires to the beautiful and brave Titans, and even Cronus – time itself. Indian creation myths have different versions. In one version, there was nothing in the beginning but a primordial being, or Hiranyagarbha. The desire to know oneself was the first seed of the mind from which everything, including the gods, were born. My personal favourite is the Native American Makiritare myth. In this myth, the woman and the man dreamt that god was dreaming them. So god was smoking, singing and dancing happily, while the man and the women dreamt that god was dreaming an egg inside which the man and the women were singing and dancing happily. Go ahead, read that line again. That's *Inception* part two right there!

Amidst the ruckus, the egg breaks and the man and the woman pop out. From then onwards they continue to live and die, and live and die and live and die endlessly. Then of course, thanks to the British Empire, we all know about the story of Adam and Eve and the seven-day creation. Many of these interesting myths of our beginning have now been discarded. With help of our added knowledge through breakthroughs in science, we now have an even better story. I would prefer stardust to puke any day.

The most popular theory asserts that our universe began with the Big Bang 14 billion years ago. It began at size zero, having infinitely high density and temperature. The universe just burst out of nothing. But how? That does not make sense! Well, apparently it does to the physics geeks. A vacuum is a 'boiling brew' of virtual particles where particles and anti-particles pop in and out of nothing and collide with each other to vanish into oblivion. 'Nothing' is not really nothing after all. There must have been a time when onwards quantum fluctuation favoured particles over anti-particles, creating matter. With matter also came energy, since, as Einstein proved, they are two sides of the same coin. While matter itself is made of positive energy, it was balanced by equal amount of negative energy that is stored in space. As the universe expanded, the temperatures dropped. This happened because the particles now had more space between them and thus less number of collisions and less heat generation. You might wonder that if time and space began with the Big Bang, what was the universe expanding into. The simple answer is that it is expanding, but it is not expanding into anything. Confused? Well, it is kind of counter-intuitive. The expanding balloon analogy does not work with the universe because there is no space outside the universe. It is same as asking what was there before the Big Bang. If time began with the Big Bang, there could be nothing before time, because 'before' does not exist without time. As the universe expands, it creates space from nothing. In other words, universe expands by creating new space. Every point in the universe is expanding since the Big Bang. Imagine the expansion not as the expansion of the whole balloon, but just the surface of it. Our entire universe is just the surface of a sphere, and hence it does not have a centre.

As temperatures dropped with further expansion, the early photons, electrons, neutrinos and their antiparticles started to form. With further drop in temperature, the strong nuclear forces became significant enough to combine photons and neutrons into atoms of deuterium. This event happened around 380,000 years after the Big Bang, which is more than the time modern humans have been roaming on earth. The deuterium combined with more protons and neutrons to form helium, along with a little bit of lithium and beryllium here and there. As the universe continued to expand and cool, gravitational attraction would become substantial and cause some regions of the universe to collapse back into itself. The gravitational forces would cause the collapsing matters to spin. In these condensed spaces, the deuterium and helium gases would collide with each other, increasing the temperature again, but this time only locally. Soon the gases would be hot enough to start nuclear fusion, resulting in the formation of the first stars. Let there be light! This process will also create newer heavier elements. Most of the gases from these stars would be blown away, and the star dusts would condense to form the planets, and eventually us.

One such planet, born 4.4 billion years ago, is our very own earth. This date comes from dating of zircon crystals from the rocks of Jack Hill in Australia. The second oldest rock happens to be from Champua in Odisha, India. These rocks of Singhbhum are 4.2 billion years old, and was reported by Dr Rajat Majumdar (along with Trisrota Chaudhuri), a brilliant professor who once taught me Geology.

One minor benefit of the greater tragedy of global warming is the new information that we are getting from the rocks that were once hidden beneath a thick pile of snow. One such lucky find was made in 2016 by a group of Australian geologists in a remote corner of Greenland. The group was led by Allen Nutman and Vickie Bennett. As they were walking over the 3.7 billion year old outcrop, they faltered upon a curious looking rock. On a closer look they saw some conical humps rising out of the flat layers in the serocks. The moment Nutmam and his team saw it, they realized that they had made a very significant discovery. Such odd but ordered structures could be sculpted by only one thing – life. The 'conical' humps looked like stromatolites. This was the eureka moment, as no one until that point of time knew that life began that early. Moreover, 3.7 billion years is too long to preserve evidence of micro life. The evidence, however, is not set in stones or rocks rather. NASA astrobiologist Abigail Allwood have claimed that the recorded 'humps' are less like 'ice cream cones' and more like 'Toblerone bars', making them 'just rocks' fashioned by tectonic forces. The jury is still out. This rock, if at all is made by life, had managed to survive the deformation like a long lost message in a bottle floating in the ocean, just to let us know. 3.7 billion years before present also coincides with the time when our Last Universal Common Ancestor (LUCA) lived. LUCA is derived from genome study of all organisms living today and back tracing the paths to a common point. Next time you see an insect in your house, remind yourself that you two are related.

How life started is still a big puzzle that needs to be cracked. Did a creator design it? Was it just a chance episode? Was it an obvious outcome of the initial conditions of our universe? In that case, why were the initial conditions just perfect enough to result in us? Or is it that we can ask these questions because we happen to be in one of the infinite universes that happen to have the right conditions for life? Unfortunately, as things stand now, we are not going to have a firm answer anytime soon. May be there is no firm answer. At least we now know that having a creator is not the only alternative. Hungarian Nobel prize winner Albert Szent-Györgyi once said, 'Life is nothing but an electron looking for a place to rest'. As long as it is 'looking', we are good. As long as the electrons are snatched and transferred from one atom to another, life will continue. There are bacteria that survive just by stripping electrons from hydrogen and attaching them into carbon dioxide, generating methane and water. That's all that living things do. Strip electrons from something and attach them to something else to tap the energy required to stay alive. Electron transfer was the first process that happened when life was born in the primordial soup, or deep-sea hydrothermal vent, or Mars, or wherever it started. In the process, life was creating information about its own identity.

Miller-Urey experiment showed that biology could be cooked out of chemistry, given the right ingredients, and a spark. Jeremy England, a biophysicist, thinks that complex structures like living things can naturally grow from restructuring effect, which he calls dissipation-driven-adaptation. Atoms try to restructure themselves in order to burn more and more energy, resulting in the rise of entropy, as required by the second law of thermodynamics. And, the most effective way of doing it is replication. However, the conditions on early earth or inside a cell are very complex and cannot be predicted from the first principles. All experiments done so far are only speculations. But one thing we know for certain, whichever way life formed, it was using geochemical energy (water-rock reactions) to survive.

The next step life required, after it was 'created', was the replication of information that made the blobs of proteins. One of the popular theories suggests that self-replicating nucleic acids were the first replicators, from which ribonucleic acid (RNA) took shape. Once the ability to replicate was learned, inanimate matter turned into living beings. Replication was the first step towards self-awareness. Recent findings propose Mars as the best place for these replicators to form. NASA's Curiosity rover found evidence of organic carbon, the building blocks of life, from 3 billion years old sedimentary rocks of Mars. Do not start jumping with joy just yet! Mars having the best conditions for initial life does not necessarily mean we are Martians.

As if creation of replicating proteins was not enough a miracle, there was an even bigger one without which there would have been no us – endosymbiosis between two prokaryotes. Biochemist Nick Lane suggests that the miracle of one bacteria getting inside another (endosymbiosis) and surviving there for generations has helped develop complex life like us. One such bacterium is the mitochondria living inside our very cells. While a single organism like LUCA giving rise to multiple organisms is undebatable, multiple organisms combining to form a single organism is more common than you imagine. Almost 40-80% of human gene arrived through ancient viral infection by the process called Lateral Gene Transfer. The genes from these archaic viruses helps us in boosting our immune system. Endosymbiosis triggered a chain of events, including formation of nucleus, sex, two sexes, predators and prey. These early forms of life were anaerobic (absence of free oxygen) microorganisms feeding on the dead cells of others. Our tiny ancestors must have been 'cannibals'. Proteins required eating proteins to survive, thus arose the first predators, and their prey. This activated the battle for survival, making way for Darwinian evolution where the fittest gene survived and spread. While the prey developed hard shell or became agile, the predators developed stronger teeth to crush their prey. Sometime before the more complex predator-prey relationship evolved, some of these early life forms learned to utilize the energy from the sun to power life. This is the time when we start finding stromatolites and banded iron formations in different parts of the globe. Evolving from anaerobic photosynthesis, life learned to take in oxygen by breaking down water molecules. This aerobic photosynthesis started to surge the oxygen content in the atmosphere, resulting in the Great Oxidation Event around 2.2 billion years ago. Red bed outcrops found around the earth are evidence of this global event. Rise of oxygen created the Ozone layer, making earth more habitable for large animals. Oxygen is the most efficient element in terms of the amount of energy released per electron transfer, apart from the much less abundant chlorine and fluorine. It was the best element available, and no wonder that it helped in the creation of complex life forms. The first single celled eukaryote evolved around 1.6 billion years ago. Eukaryotes are special, because they were the first life form to have sex. Instead of just copying itself with all the errors, sex helped in mixing of genetic materials between partners. We exist because these ancient life forms found a way to survive and transfer their genes to their next generation. Evolution was now spoiled for choice.

The oxygen level kept rising. It rose rapidly to modern day concentrations during Snowball Earth that happened around 750-600 million years ago. The vast oceans absorbed the free oxygen. Conditions were now ideal for the earliest known complex multicellular organisms, called Ediacarans, to evolve. A recent analysis of fat molecules found from Russia of a specific type of Ediacarans named Dickinsonia, conclusively proves for the first time that these mysterious species are actually large and pretty abundant animals. Multicellular organisms developed special systems, like the nervous system, that helped them sense the world in a more advanced way than their unsophisticated ancestors. The nerve cells clustered together in some part of the body to form the primitive brains. This created desires that helped the organisms to survive and reproduce. After a pause for a century or so since the first Ediacarans, life began to explode. This period, as recorded in the fossils in rocks of around 541 million years ago, is known as the Cambrian explosion. This was the beginning of a new episode in the history of living beings. The best evidence of Cambrian explosion in India is preserved in the Blue City of Rajasthan. We went to Jodhpur as part of a field trip to look at the rock outcrops and understand the reservoirs that host the largest on land oil discovery of India. In the surrounding area there were some older rocks called the Jodhpur sandstones. The pink Jodhpur sandstones are too old and too tight to interest oil hunters, however they would fascinate any geologist. These famous sandstones have been queried and the slabs sold as building materials all over the world. While we are losing these rocks rapidly, it also gave us the opportunity to look at some fresh rock faces. In one of those fresh rock faces were some bizarre disk-shaped fossils. This is how our ancestors looked 540 million years ago! These discoidal fossils are the most common and youngest Ediacaran fossils in the world. Since Cambrian, life has never looked back.

The first dominant vertebrates were the prehistoric fishes that swam the ancient ocean 500 to 400 million years ago. From these 'fishes' evolved the adventurous tetrapods. They were the first animals to get out of the ocean and colonize the dry lands, around 400 million years ago. For the next 50 million years, the amphibians dominated the land and had the better of the modest reptiles. Evolution has a twisted sense of humour, and soon the tables were turned. The reptiles grew big and became the glamorous dinosaurs, while the amphibians shrunk into frogs and toads. Our tiny furry warm-blooded ancestors evolved around 230 million years ago. They lived under the shadows of the mighty dinosaurs. While these first mammals were no match for the giant reptiles, they were the masters of hiding, running, and most importantly, surviving. Our ancestors survived what even the dinosaurs could not – the K-T extinction that wiped out 75% of all species. As the reptile menace perished, it was time for the mammals to flourish. The brains of mammals developed a special area dedicated to filial emotions that helped them bind with each other. Unity was the key to mammals' survival. Primates evolved from the tree hugging mammals of the tropical forests. They were the most social of all animals, and the social emotions like guilt and pride became a dominant part of their brain. Emotions, however, was not their dominant strength. It was intelligence that made apes class apart. Who knew what these innocent looking animals would soon be up to and where they would be larking around?

The smart ape

The evolution towards *Homo sapiens* began more than 30 million years ago, 200 kms below the surface of earth, at a temperature of 1500°c, somewhere under the Mountain of Moon. That was where a dangerous force was unleashed, that changed the world forever. The heat 200 kms below the earth (geologists calls it magma plume), was slowly tearing Africa apart (rifting). The force that was soon going to change our fate was first changing the geography of East Africa. The landscape slowly evolved into The Great African Rift Valley. It created deep lakes like the 1470m deep Lake Tanganyika, and the high mountains like the 5109m tall Mt Rwenzori, all within next 20 million years. The high mountains blocked the clouds, creating a rain shadow in the eastern part of Africa, making it more arid and forcing some apes to start walking on two feet. A kilometer reduction of topography would have meant I would not have been here to write this book, the world would have been a lot greener, and we would not have been worried about global warming.

The single most important thing that separates us from other primates is our ability to walk upright. In 1976, Mary Leakey and her team discovered hominin fossil footprints preserved in an ancient volcanic ash layer of Tanzania. A trio of *Australopithecus afarensis* walked over the soft volcanic ash bed. One of them was possibly carrying a baby. Soon, more volcanic ash rained down and preserved the prints. These 'Laetoli Footprints' within 3.6 million years old rocks are the oldest evidence of bipedalism. The colossal change of climate initiated by the tectonic forces most likely triggered the evolution of apes. The climate in which our ancestors became so comfortable, changed from rainforests to savannas. These changes meant that the apes themselves had to change to adapt to the new conditions. One such change was the decision to walk upright. The reduction of trees meant that our ancestors were forced to come down from the comfort of the trees down to the unsafe ground. What actually influenced bipedalism is debatable, but it gave us a colossal advantage. Bipedalism is effective in terms of energy conservation, making us more agile. It not only helped us catch prey, but also helped us run away from the predators. But the most significant aspect of bipedalism was that it freed our hands. We were now ready to take our, and along with that the rest of the planet's, future into our own hands. The use of tools required hand-eye coordination, fine motor skill development, and processing of large volumes of information that required a powerful brain. Bipedalism happened about 5 million years ago and it corresponds to the time when our direct ancestor's brain began to develop, not just in size but also complexity. Desires were the first to develop in living beings, followed by emotions in the mammals. Now the third and the most powerful part of the brain was evolving – intelligence.

The next big step our ancestors took was the control of fire. It was in fact control over one's fear. The oldest evidence of primates consciously controlling fire dates back to 1.7 million years, but the definitive evidence is from 600,000 years ago by *Homo erectus*. By 125,000 years, anatomically modern humans became masters of controlling fire. Fire gave us a big advantage over other animals. It warmed us at night and helped us colonize colder places. The 'red flower' also helped us scare predators and cook prey. Fire not only assisted us forge better weapons, it also abetted us create works of art like terracotta statues and pottery. Not to forget, candle light dinners. Had we not been playing with fire, mammoths would still be around, and we would probably be in the caves. The cooked food was healthy as it killed unhealthy bacteria like *E.Coli* and salmonella. Cooked food was also easier to digest. As a consequence, our stomach, teeth and mouth became smaller and there was decrease in the size of our gastrointestinal track and organs in the digestive system. British Primatologist Richard Wrangh am suggests that the brains now used this freed up energy to grow. Change in food habit, like increase in meat and shellfish consumption, increased dopamine secretion in the brain, making us smarter. The intelligent human beings had a better chance of survival and were more efficient at finding mates. Humans with genes that made them intelligent bred more and rapidly spread in the population by natural selection.

Just when all seemed to be going well for our species, we had a problem – the problem of our growing head. Our brain was adding 150 million brain cells every hundred thousand years as we evolved from just another ape to the inquisitive ape. However, the bigger brain did come at a cost. While being just 2% of our body weight, human brains consume 20% of our energy requirement, much higher than any other animal. This increased our food requirement, keeping the intelligent us busier than the stupider ones. Had we been a bit less smart, the world would have a lot more food. More energy for the brain meant that there was less energy to build muscles. Our intelligence came at the cost of our strength. Then again, who needs strength when you can fool both your prey and predators? The large brains also meant a large skull to contain it. This made childbirth difficult, painful and even fatal. The birth canal of women had to grow wider to adjust to the bigger skull. But it was not enough, as the brain of the primates of *'homo'* genus continued to grow. The solution was in giving early birth, before the skull became too big. The complex brain also required more time to mature, increasing our childhood. Despite the common sentiment that our carefree happy youthful days passed in a hurry, we can consider ourselves lucky because childhood is much shorter for other animals. The need to take care of infants, who were born early and immature, for a longer period of time may have bonded the parents together. Partners in love stayed together and cared for their offspring. The brains could now continue to grow, but it made these primates less mobile. They stayed in one place for a long time. However, the benefits of a large brain far outweighed the costs. Intelligence gifted humans the ability of 'behavioural plasticity' instead of special 'hard-wired' abilities. We adapted easily with the environment and became the fittest of all competitors.

The most significant invention of the 'smart' us was language. It probably evolved from imitation of gestures or sounds of grunts and clicks. Clicks are still part of many languages like the Khoisan languages of Africa where it is used as consonants. This new found tool of language not only helped in communication, but also in making and sharing stories. Language has the power to shape the way you think. To the Spanish, a bridge is 'strong' while for the German, a bridge is 'beautiful'. Why? Because in German language, a bridge is feminine, and in Spanish, it is masculine. The description of the bridge fits our gender stereotypes. The way you speak guides the way you think. But why was it that of all species, only *Homo sapiens* developed complex form of language?

Invention of language was a cognitive revolution for our species, which could well have been activated by some sort of mutation. Noam Chomsky's theory of generative grammar is based on the idea that all languages in the world share a common set of rules. This can be described along six dimensions: structural principle, physical mechanisms, manner of use, ontogenetic development, phylogenetic development, and integration of animal signaling. This rule is ingrained in our genes. One must not get carried away here to believe that we are the only species that communicate using language. We know of birds like parrots that can make sounds just like us. A whale can communicate meaningful words using sonic waves with another whale that is hundreds of kilometres away. Green monkeys have different words to differentiate between 'Careful Lion!' and 'Careful Eagle!' The former warning will make them climb up the tree, while the later will make them jump down. Both the warnings together would just mean that they are having a really bad day. Baboons have at least 14 different vocalizations that we know of, to mean 14 different things. Interestingly, the area of our brain that is associated with speech is the same area responsible for singing in zebra finches. Does that mean language is in our genes?

Research has found a link between FOXP2 gene with the evolution of human speech and language. Mutation of this gene not just results in speech impairment in humans, but also lack of singing ability in flinches. Unlike other animals, humans have developed a very complex language that can go beyond warning and singing. Other animals communicate about immediate danger, while we can teach dangers of predators to our kids through stories even before they face a real threat. We can talk and plan ahead to save ourselves from predators, while at the same time strategizing how to kill our next prey. We can gossip about whom you like and whom you don't, about who is helpful and who is a cheater, about who loves whom and who is sleeping with whom. Yuval Noah Harari believes that none of these 'fictions' would have been possible without language. This great cognitive revolution happened around 70,000 years ago.

Unlike animals, culture binds a large group of people together through an idea that does not exist in reality. Such ideas have been termed as mnemes. The mnemes exists because of language. Languages are random vibrations whose pattern we associate with a certain meaning. The sounds are abstract, as it does not have any real universal meaning. Its meaning only exists in our mind once we are trained to do so. Language, however, creates bonds between large groups of people that define a culture. The same is true for religion. It helps create an identity, a sense of unity, which has historically helped tribes to survive in the wild. Nationalism is also same as religion. Instead of an imaginary faith, we now have the idea of imaginary borders that only exists in the human mind. It makes you believe that your country is the best just because you happen to be born in it. What are the odds of that happening? Politics is no different. The leaders who create history, most often than not, are people who were able to incept their ideas in the minds of a large group of individuals; individuals, who were ready to fight and die for that idea. Ideas are stories you believe in, some of which might lead to an easier life for many. One such idea is equality. It does not mean anything to the universe. Equality does not exist in nature. It is a human creation. This story is a good one for many of us because it helps the weaker people of the society survive. It is just an idea nevertheless, an idea that many people believe in. Ideas have resulted in numerous battles and bloodshed, ideas have annihilated Hiroshima and Nagasaki, and ideas now breed terrorism. Ideas have also given us art and literature, built civilizations, and created artificial intelligence. Without language, there would have been no ideas, and without ideas we would have remained as just another ape. It was language that gave us moral uplift and edification.

The term 'language' is derived from Latin word *lingua*, which literally means 'tongue'. The ability to speak comes from more than just the fleshy muscular organ. The vocal tract structures that helps us speak also includes the larynx, the neck (that houses the vocal cords), and the pharynx (a tube that rises above the larynx and opens into the oral and nasal cavities). Based on fossil records we can convincingly say that this anatomy existed since 600,000 years ago. We had the ability to create sound over half a million years before we actually started speaking. There must have been a distinct evolutionary advantage that created our vocal tract, because it came at a heavy cost. Most mammals, including baby humans, have the larynx positioned high, resulting in short pharynx. This limits vocal modulation and thus speaking. As we become adults, our pharynx length increases and the larynx is pushed further down in the neck. This helps us make a variety of sounds. But, this also means that we cannot breathe and swallow at the same time, increasing our chance of choking to death. This adaptation must have some strong benefit like better breathing. The vocal tract configuration stayed as an exaptation like the feathers of birds. Feathers' original purpose was to insulate, only later it became useful for flying. In the same way, our vocal tract evolved due to a genetic copying error and had some beneficial purpose that it stayed with us. Its real use came much later when humans were migrating out of Africa.

The time of migration out of Africa, also known as the 'Great Leap Forward', roughly accords with climate change resulting from the great Toba eruption. Recent findings do suggest that there might have been older migrations and intermixing with other hominids. The lethal eruption that occurred 70,000 years ago, created a ten-year-long winter. It was an ecological disaster that destroyed almost all of the vegetation. The long and harsh winter decreased the human population of the world to just

3,000-10,000 individuals, almost erasing the traces of older migration. Yes, you heard right. At one point of time, we were almost as dead as the dodo. All human beings alive today are descendants from those small numbers of individuals, as proven by genetic studies. In fact, every person alive in this world today can be traced back to a single female who lived 140,000 years ago and to a single male living 90,000 years ago. Language would have come in very handy during these trying times. It might have been possible that the groups that did not communicate well, perished. This might be a reason why the estimated Cognitive Revolution coincides with this Toba erruption.

It was language that led to the symbol-centric behaviour of modern Cro-Magnons. This symbol-centric behaviour spread through cultural diffusion around the globe. It was easy to learn, as our brains and the vocal chords were already up for it. While animals are intuitive, human beings' mix of intuition and symbolism has created art and innovation. Language not just gives us the ability to communicate, but also write down our ideas and stories. This gives us the ability to learn from our ancestors and build on to the past knowledge. While other animals only have genetic memory that becomes their instincts, we evolve through collective memory of huge information database at a much rapid pace, making us potentially dangerous, and pushing us to the top of the food chain. Still, there is a significant data loss, and isolated ideas die. But, in the future, with internet connectivity and ability to store huge information, the data loss would become negligible. The potential pace with which our future generation can develop with all that information is unimaginable.

Once our ancestors were out of the comfort of their ancestral home in Africa, they required innovation to survive. The more risks they took, the more they ended up making new discoveries. These new adventures were having a profound effect on their brains. *Homo sapiens* were evolving into a perfect predator. The cave paintings by early sapiens revealed their love for hunting, music, and dancing. As the ice age melted away and the earth became more hospitable; people started getting organized into groups and settled down in a fertile land. Agriculture led to significant surplus in food production, resulting in accelerated population growth. People used the extra time to create art, craft and ultimately trading. The transition to agrarian lifestyle was not a sudden revolution that happened around 10,000 years ago. It was a gradual change occurring over thousands of years. With agriculture, human beings started to tweak the rules of nature. In nature, the big fish eats small fish, and the fittest survive. Humans created a world where even the weak could survive. Our ancestors tamed the wild and laid the foundation of our modern civilization. But why did civilization not spring up in all parts of the world at the same time?

Jared Diamond writes in his book *Guns, Germs, and Steel* that the spread of food production through a long east-west axis like Europe to Asia was easy. The same was difficult along the long north-south axis of America or Africa as climate changed quickly over short distances across different latitudes. A single innovation in one place rapidly spread along the east–west axis. It helped in development of trading, technologies, pottery, metallurgy, writing, etc., in Eurasia. Genetic diversity is the greatest along this axis of Eurasia as compared to the north-south axis of America or Africa. Birds of the same feather flock together and people of the same weather, well, fall in love together. This easy diffusion acted as a catalyst in the progress of human civilization in the 'Cradle of Civilization', while other continents failed to catch up.

To create large civilization, human beings had to go against their very nature. The human mind cannot maintain social relationship with more than 10 to 200 individuals. This limitation is called the Dunbar's Number and is guided by the size of the neo-cortex. Larger groups that happened with the rise of civilizations needed a tool, an idea, to bind people together. The idea came in the form of society and religion. Such ideas created new rules of survival. While it created groups that believed in a particular fiction, it also created the difference between groups who believed in different fictions which were often not compatible with each other. The logos of intelligence and mythos of emotions was growing together with desires for the first time in any species. From the single cells of Isua and Akiliawe almost miraculously evolved into a complex organism that can read and write. The tortuous path of human evolution created culture. But is culture powerful enough to change the course of our evolution?

Culture and evolution

Desires, emotions and intelligence have shaped human history. Arts, languages, religions, nationalism and politics are outcomes of history that define cultures. Culture is unique to human beings if you define it as a complex social organization where people learn shared way of life transmitted through symbolic forms of communication, like language. Language, as discussed earlier, is rooted in our genes. In fact gene and culture influence each other and evolve together. The idea of gene and culture co-evolution goes back to Charles Darwin. Richard Dawkins, in his book *The Selfish Genes*, introduced the idea of cultural evolution. Later, scientists like E.O. Wilson, mathematically proved the existence of gene-culture co-evolution. It is now popularly known as the Dual Inheritance Theory (DIT). The closest example of DIT in animals is probably the domestication of dogs. Few wolves got friendly with some human tribes, probably for easy food. The creepier wolves were scared off or hunted down, while the ones with gentler traits received food and shelter. The friendly wolves had a better chance of survival and bred more under the protection of humans. Over time, the wild wolves turned into cuddly tail-wagging dogs. If cultural habit can impact other animals, can it influence humans too?

Human beings accumulate ideas and technologies over generations and culture evolves. A group's preference of fire is part of the group's culture. Inventions like fire, or stone tools gave few groups of individuals the advantage of survival. The groups that did not learn the new inventions perished, while the genes of those that survived dominated. Evolution by natural selection happens in these small steps of elimination. Genetics have influenced our history, and history has influenced our culture. But who would have thought that culture can itself affect our genes. There was a time when humans could not digest cow's milk. Once we started domesticating cows, our digestive system evolved in a way that it became easier to digest milk, or milk products. It started with a few groups of individuals, somewhere in Slovakia, Poland and Hungary, in whom there was a mutation that made them lactose tolerant. The mutation was a result of a single letter gene in LCT gene that happened between 5,000 to 10,000 BCE. Interestingly, lactose tolerance mutation happened in Africa and Asia later, because of a different mutation. Cow's milk became an easy source of protein and fat that gave the animal herders better chance of survival compared to hunters and gatherers. These new mutants thus spread more rapidly than the ones who could not digest milk. Today there are so many people around the world who can drink milk without the fear of dying. Culture guides our evolution and decides which genes will spread and which will be eliminated. Those who inherit characters that help them follow the prevalent culture, which includes religion and nationalism, survive and reproduce more than those who do not.

The physical or behavioural trait that is preferred by the dominant culture in a group would determine the genes that would spread rapidly. These genes would in turn guide the physical and behavioural trait of future generations. There is a feedback mechanism at play. These traits could be entirely imaginary bias like skin colour or height. Within a couple of centuries, the Dutch, once known for their short height, became world's tallest people. As per the Dutch military records, the average height of the Dutch men has grown by 20 cms in the last 150 years. Wealth and better nutrition has also been seen in other countries and is not enough to explain such rapid increase in height. Consistent with the most accepted hypothesis, the Dutch men owe their height to the preference of Dutch women for tall men. It was found that tall men had more children than shorter ones. Dutch women preferred tall men and thus the gene for 'tallness' spread amongst the Dutch population. Natural selection was at play, and it was guided by cultural preference. For natural selection to be effective, a cultural preference should persist for a long time. A historical event, like colonialism, can create a biased culture, like preference of white skin, which can trigger natural selection and redirect the line of evolution. The stories that dominate our culture will guide the future of our species. In fact, some cultural changes can even leave an epigenetic imprint on the DNA. It acts like memory and is genetically transferred to the next kin. Genes encodes the RNAs to build proteins that regulate humans who sense the environment and cultures that influence the epigenomes, which in turn regulates the genes. What we are today, is a result of combination of selfish desires, cultural emotions, and intelligent tactics.

How we came to be?

A pes evolved miraculously from the specs of dusts created during the Big Bang, which itself was created from nothing. Human beings happen to be one such ape. At this moment in earth's history, we are probably the most successful species, after bacteria. But we are also very lucky to be where we are. We are a product of random events and lucky escapes rather than a grand plan. There are still a lot of questions that are unanswered, like what was there before the Big Bang (may be inflation, may be not), how exactly living beings, or consciousness, came from the non-living or why is there anything at all? No one knows. There is no way to deny that there was a creator who created everything and then rested. Even the theory of natural selection has loopholes. However, the gaps in the alternative theories are much larger. Evidence of evolution can be found within your body. Hiccups are a reminder that we had a fishy ancestor. Our ears still have traces of evidence of evolving from fish jaws. Science has managed to understand quite a bit of how life works, but not why it came to be. That does not mean by default that there was an invisible hand. Not having an answer is better than a wrong answer.

The strength of our species lies in its complex brain that has three components – desire, emotion and intelligence. Desire was the first to evolve in animals to help meet the basic needs of food, sex and shelter. Strong emotional bonds evolved next in the mammals. Emotion glued our species together. Intelligence became the powerful trait of the primates, and it became a dominant part of the human mind. The key trait of intelligence is our ability to interpolate and extrapolate information (memory), and more importantly, classify that information into arbitrary pigeon holes. Our symbol-centric brain helps us quickly judge a situation and react to it. Quick reaction time was often a matter of life and death for our ancestors. Extrapolation of information helps us predict and plan ahead. However, the interpolation and extrapolation of information is often fiction because you create a hypothetical situation that has not happened, and react to eliminate any possible threat that is yet to take place. This changed the whole game of evolution. According to the old tried and tested formula, prey became scarier to survive. Predators stayed away from animals that looked poisonous. Humans, on the other hand, try to eliminate such threats even when they are not directly threatened. If snakes are poisonous, other animals will stay away from it. We, on the other hand will find innovative ways to eliminate the poor snake. If the tiger is a threat, we will go and hunt it down, display it in our drawing room, and bring it to the brink of extinction, and not hide from it. Evolution has turned us into a powerful killing machine. To survive in the new human-dominated world, wolves have to turn to friendly dogs. Now dogs have a better chance of survival than wolves. At the same time, we have created a civilization that leads to survival of even the weakest humans, despite few horrific events in history. We all are familiar with the different policies of Nazi Germany to drive genetic 'purity' and create 'better' humans. Even before the Nazis, way back in 1904, US scientists created a campaign to improve their gene pool by forced sterilization of people who they considered 'dumb' and 'feeble minded'. Luckily, all such attempts have ended in failure. The power of creating fiction has not just helped us climb to the top of the food chain, but has also given us this remarkable ability to gossip, weave stories, and create myths, legends, gods, currencies, nations, morality, and everything that makes up a civilization. Intelligence gives us this uncanny knack of asking questions and trying to make sense of everything we know. But how?

Question 2

How Do We Make Sense of the Universe Around Us?

'No two people see the external world in exactly the same way. To every separate person a thing is what he thinks it is - in other words, not a thing, but a think.'

– Penelope Fitzgerald, *The Gate of Angels* (1990)

Re-assembling a broken egg

The moment Harish Bhimani's voice boomed out of the television set, *'Main Samay hoon'* (I am time), we used to rush towards the TV room. As the wheel of time revolved, we got glued to the black and white Konark television set to watch one of our all-time favourite TV soaps – *Mahabharat*. Time is something we are so familiar with. We get angry when it is wasted, we curse ourselves for not having enough of it; there are bad times; time is money and it flies too; there are good times and then there is (or was) the king of good times. Time is priceless and free. You can't own it, but you can use it. You can't keep it, but you can spend it. Once you've lost it, you can never get it back. That is a lot of clichés for one paragraph. When I started to dig up more information on time, I realized how little I knew about it. What is time? Does it have a beginning or an end? Is it a fundamental entity? Why do we only remember the past? Unless we find answers to these questions, it would be difficult to understand how we perceive the universe.

Wikipedia defines time as 'a part of the measuring system used to sequence events, to compare the durations of events and the intervals between them, and to quantify rates of change such as the motions of objects.' Time exists because of change. If there is no change, there is no time. Einstein has shown that time is just another dimension of space. It was 1904 and he was just 26 years old, when his revelation changed physics forever. Einstein proved that time is not an absolute entity, and the way we experience time is relative. This came to be known as the Special Theory of Relativity. Light travels at the same speed, i.e. 299,792,458 m/s (in vacuum) irrespective of the speed you are travelling at. If that does not sound strange, then think about this. Let's say that both you and I are travelling at different speeds in two different cars, and we both are looking at the same tree outside. So, we are both moving at different relative velocities with respect to that tree. However, if that tree was a photon, then it would have the same relative velocity with respect to both you and me, irrespective of what our velocities were. No matter how fast you run, you can never catch it. So, two persons travelling at different speeds sees the same light travelling at the speed of 299,792,458 m/s. Light having constant velocity, and the fact that the change of distance of both you and me from the photon is different, the distance and time for both of us has to be different. Time gets slower for the person travelling faster. This shocked the world because it was not how time was perceived. Time was supposed to be same for everyone and everything in all corners of the universe, consistent with common sense Newtonian Physics. Common sense is not always correct. Recent experiments with high resolution instruments have proven that time dilates and space contracts at higher speeds. In fact, you are probably using this theory every day. The GPS in your smart phone communicates with the satellites in the orbit that tick a bit faster than your time. Your phone is programmed to adjust that time dilation. The time and space on which our perception of life depends so much is indeed fluid, like in the dream world. If you travel at 99% the speed of light, your 10 years will be equivalent to 70 years for the people on earth. This would also mean that people at different latitudes in the world, who are moving at different relative velocities (along with the different tectonic plate velocities, gravity and earth's wobble), must age as per a different time clock.

Some physicists have learnt from black holes that the real physical processes are happening within the thin surface of our closed universe. Whatever we observe, being within the volume, is a just a projection of that reality. So time (and space), as we know it, is not a reality and depends on what is happening in the distant outer space. This is called the holographic principle of string theory and was first proposed by Gerard 't Hooft. If that is true, it would mean that we have no free will; it is the process in the surface of our universe that controls our future that is pre-determined. As per this theory, space-time is a secondary phenomenon, a large-scale manifestation of some fundamental entity. No one knows what that entity is, but one thing is for certain, time as we know it is just an illusion. Time is just another dimension of space and, like distance, it is relative. Explain that to your partner when you are late for a date. After that, either you will never be late for a date, or you will never go on a date. But,why does time travel only from past to future when there are no such mathematical restrictions to it?

Italian theoretical physicist Carlo Rovelli suggests that time does not exist at all. It is just the space between 'memory and anticipation'. Rovelli and Conne's 'Thermal Time Hypothesis' states that the universe is made of countless events, and the flow of time is just an illusion. Physical laws would probably not mind if you go back in time to that date with your partner and change your decision to explain to her that time is relative. Unfortunately, you are not that lucky. One possible reason is that the initial conditions during the Big Bang had been low entropy. The entropy was so low that it can only increase with time (second law of thermodynamics), making time unidirectional. At least for the moment. Hence, the probability of creating an order out of chaos is very less. Consider an 8 volume book. There are 40,320 (8 x 7 x 6 x 5 x 4 x 3 x 2 x 1) different ways in which you can arrange it. Only one of them is in an ordered state (volume 1 to volume 8), and the rest 40,329 are in a disordered state. So there is very less chance of the books to fall in an ordered state if you randomly throw them on the floor. Similarly, there is very less chance that a smashed egg will return to its unbroken state, no matter how hard you try. Even all the kings' horses and all the kings' men failed. To make it possible, the reverse has to be perfect even at the atomic scale. That is one success out of billions of other failed disordered states. Theoretically it is possible to reassemble the egg atom by atom, but if you have broken it, try making an omelette instead. In case of the outside chance of the egg reassembling itself, you will forget that you broke it anyway. Theoretical physicist Lorenzo Maccone found out in his study that the entropy can decrease as well, but the process would destroy any evidence of its existence. When the entropy of the system decreases, the 'quantum mutual information' (whatever that is) also reduces, in a process erasing the memory! If this theory is correct, there is no way you can remember the future. So the future is kind of Las Vegas. What happens there, stays there. If no one remembers the future, it never happened!

While time itself is complicated, our perception of time also varies. It depends on our emotions, memory and even our body temperature. Fear is an evolutionary emotion that helps us survive. It also makes us more attentive, resulting in an increase in the amount of data that gets stored in our memory while we are afraid. This creates the illusionas if time is getting dragged. Neuroscientist David Eagleman experimentally demonstrated this phenomenon of how fear slows down our time. You can only pity the participants who dared to be part of his experiment. Memory is kind of related to the first cause. More the memories one makes, slower the time passes for him or her. This is called time wrap. The third cause is the surprising one. Psychologist Hudson Hoagland realized that time seems to slow down when one has fever, after his sick wife kept complaining that he was staying away from him for too long. Surprised by her behaviour, he studied her a bit more and came to the conclusion that the higher her body temperature was, slower the time went for her. Later, he performed the same experiment on a student by artificially raising his body temperature and came to the same conclusion. Time perception varies from human to human, and also dramatically between animals. It depends on how rapidly the nervous system of the animal processes the information. Some experiments suggest that smaller and lighter animals with higher metabolic rate perceive time at a finer resolution. Life seems to move in slow motion for them. Which means that they can do more in less time. Having a shorter life span does not necessarily mean a short life!

Despite the confusion in measuring time, our body has an internal time clock that guides us through the day. It tells us when to eat our food and when to go to sleep. If you break your internal time clock, you can land yourself in serious health troubles, which includes obesity, mental illness and even cancer. Three scientists Jeffrey C. Hall, Michael Rosbash and Michael W. Young were awarded the 2017 Nobel Prize in Physiology or Medicine for proving just that. They discovered the molecular mechanisms controlling the internal body clock, or circadian rhythm. Studying fruit flies, they have identified the gene responsible for the body clock. They called it the 'period' gene. One may wonder what a fruit fly has to do with us. You would be surprised to know how similar we are. Sharmila Bhattacharya of NASA tells us that, 'about 61% of known human disease genes have a recognizable match in the genetic code of fruit flies, and 50% of fly protein sequences have mammalian analogues.' Humans too have the 'period' gene which helps secrete a protein at night that degrades during the day, helping our body keep track of time. This cycle is governed by light and is distorted by irregular lifestyle. Getting into a healthy lifestyle that matches our natural cycle is the key to a healthy life.

Quantum Maya

I hope the readers can now begin to appreciate how complicated and counter-intuitive the universe is, and how our brain create simple stories to make sense of the complicated universe. Let me dwell on this point a bit further. The discoveries of Newton and Maxwell are generally considered as the two pillars of Classical Physics. One explained what holds us bound to the ground, and the other showed us the relation between electricity, magnetism and light. At that point of time, it seemed like we knew everything about the ocean of knowledge. Simon Laplace presumed that all that was now required was unlimited computing power and knowledge of disposition of all particles at some instant of time to predict future and retrodict the past. Lord Kelvin, in the 19th century, made the bold claim that all big ideas of physics were now known. Even Max Planck, in the early

20th century, was discouraged from taking up a subject that had nothing of any worth left to discover. Fortunately, he ignored the suggestions. Soon his discovery that radiation was emitted or absorbed from time to time in packets of energy of definite size (quanta) instead of oozing continuously, challenged the fundamentals of classical physics.

Not long after, a third class examiner in the Patent Office in Berne, a genius named Einstein, discovered that the number of electrons knocked off a metallic plate by a beam of light depended more on its frequency than intensity. Einstein's results matched with those of Plank – the amount of energy in a quantum of light is proportional to its frequency. Einstein later received the Nobel Prize for his explanation of the photoelectric effect. This gave Physics a new riddle to solve – was light a wave or particle? This was just the beginning. Classical physics received the ultimate shock from Rutherford's experiments. By passing alpha particles through thin gold film, he demonstrated that the atoms were like our solar system, where the electrons rotated around the nucleus. This created a heck of a problem for the physicists. If the electrons are encircling the nucleus, then there would be decay of energy and the electrons would collapse towards the centre! What stopped them from collapsing, if not god? This is where Niels Bohr, who was working with Rutherford in Manchester, came to the rescue.

Taking a clue from Planks discrete package, Bohr proposed that the radii of revolution of the individual electrons too had discrete values, instead of it being continuous. When electrons revolved in these permitted energy shells, there was no decay of energy. If the electrons happen to lose or gain energy, they would move only from one permitted shell to another. But why would there be such a preference? The electrons turned out to be more mysterious. J.J. Thomson once won the Nobel Prize for proving that electrons were particles. Ironically, his son George Thomson, along with Louis de Broglie, won the Nobel Prize for demonstrating that electrons behaved like a wave as well. Electrons had to behave as wave in order to exist only at specific frequencies or energy shells. They went on to suggest that all matter had wave properties. The riddle of wave-particle duality was not just restricted to light. The era of Quantum Mechanics dawned with the attempt at solving this key riddle. Physicists like Broglie, Bohr, Heisenberg, Schrödinger and Dirac became the pioneers of this new era. It was not the end of Physics after all. We were just standing on the shores of knowledge when we thought we had concurred it all.

Since the boom of Quantum Mechanics and the experimental proof of our weird life, philosophers have started showing interest in physics. This is especially true for the Asian philosophies, which strike a chord with the results of quantum experiments. Even scientists like Fritjof Capra have tried to link the scientific results with Asian philosophies. Quite naturally, Quantum Mechanics has been used, and mostly misused, widely in an attempt to rationalize ancient philosophies, scriptures, and eventually, religion. One must not forget that the gap between science and philosophy was much narrower in the past than it is today, and it was even more so for the East than for the West. The main reason for such a gap was that western classical science has always held observation and experiments at higher regard than thought experiments and philosophies. Thoughts, to them, were just imagination, while experiments were reality. Advent of Quantum Mechanics changed that narrative. Our thoughts were more powerful than previously realized and the experiments questioned the very fabric of our reality, thus narrowing down the gap once more. Quantum Mechanics is difficult to grasp and is very counter intuitive. There are only few people in the world who truly understand it, and I am not one of them. However, this chapter would be incomplete without Quantum Mechanics. So, I will make the bold attempt of discussing few of the fascinating aspects of this startling branch of physics.

The quest to unravel the mysteries of nature has never been stronger than it is in the current century. Scientists are in a mad rush to find the 'Theory of Everything' – the single unified theory that will decode the mind of 'god'. The theory has evaded scientists for centuries. The advent of Quantum Mechanics took us closer to our aspiration, but not before making us realize that the actual goal is further than we ever thought. The double-slit experiment had revolutionized science and unraveled the mystery of our universe that once physicists thought we knew all about. You might lose your sanity trying to think of it, but it is true. Experiments have proved time and again that the photons, electrons and other quantum particles can behave either as wave or as particles, and their behaviour changes depending upon whether we are observing it or not. Let me explain the experiment to make things more clear. Consider two parallel walls with the first wall having two slits. Now you throw a ball through one of the slits to hit the second wall. The ball hits the second wall and leaves a mark. As you keep throwing more and more balls through the two slits randomly, there will be two parallel areas on the second wall with the ball marks, one for each slit. That is exactly how particles behave. Now, in place of particles, if waves/ripples of water passed through the slits, it will split into two waves, one passing through each slit. The two waves would interact with each other on the other side of the wall and create an interference pattern. If we could record the wave amplitude that hits the second wall, the constructive and destructive interference would result in a series of bright and dark lines instead of just two lines.

In the quantum experiment, electrons (or photons) were passed through the slits and then recorded in a detector to understand if they behaved as wave or particle. The electrons were shot through the slits, one by one. Even though the electrons were not interfering with each other because they were not fired together, there was an interference pattern! This would be possible only if the electron was a wave and passed through both slits at once when fired, just like ripples in water. This is called a superposition and not really the weird part. To understand which slit the electrons passed through to create interference, the scientists put a detector, like a strong source of light, near the slits. When the electron passes through a particular slit it scattered the light making a flash at the slit through which it passed. If it passed through both slits at the same time, there would be flash of light at both slits. The moment the electrons were observed with the help of detectors, the interference pattern did not exist anymore. There were just two lines. The electrons behaved like particles. That surprised the physicists. Maybe the lights were interfering with the experiment in some way. So, different experiments were done to eliminate errors.

But each and every time the experiments confirmed this strange phenomenon. This was not an experimental error. The very act of measurement changed the results. But how did the particles know that they were being watched?

To make sense of this creepy conclusion, scientists tried a variation of the double-slit experiment. They measured the second electron passing through the slit after the first one had already hit the screen. So the first ones would show wave pattern, and second one should behave as a particle. This experiment was originally proposed by John Wheeler in 1970, and was known as Delayed Choice Experiment. Advancement of technology made it possible later to conduct Wheeler's thought experiment. It has been done many times, including recently by physicists in Australian National University. Again, without detection during the entire experiment, the electrons behaved as wave, and when observed, all the electrons behaved as particle. This is where it gets real weird. All the electrons, even the ones fired before the measurement, knew what the scientists were up to and chose its place in the screen accordingly. Observing the electron after few have already passed through the slit gave perfect two lines and not a mixture of two lines and interference, as one would expect. How could the first electron know that the second one will be detected at some time in the future, and already behaved accordingly in advance? Interestingly, if you tag the electron while they pass through the slit and erase the tag before it hits the wall, then again you get the interference pattern back. So, the particles not just knew that we were observing, but also knew that we will be observing them or not in the future. What does that say about the arrow of time? Two-state-vector formalism

(TSVF) states that Quantum Mechanics works the same way, both forward and backward in time, thus cause can propagate backward in time and occur after its affect. Confused? You are in good company. Niels Bohr once said, 'If Quantum Mechanics hasn't profoundly shocked you, you haven't understood it yet.' After the extraordinary discoveries by Quantum Mechanics, I can safely say, truth is indeed stranger than even science fiction. This reminds me of what Hamlet said to Horatio, 'There are more things in heaven and earth, Horatio/Than are dreamt of in your philosophy.'

There are many popular theories of Quantum Mechanics that explain this weirdness. The oldest and the most popular one is the classic Copenhagen interpretation devised by Niels Bohr and Werner Heisenberg between 1925 and 1927. So far, quantum realm is known to exist only at micro scale. At larger scale, it quickly decapitates by a phenomenon called decoherence. In the Copenhagen interpretation, physical systems do not have a fixed property before measurement, but it exists in a set of probabilities. The probability wave of all possible results collapse into a single reality when observed, a process known as wave function collapse. It means that we live mostly outside the realm of weirdness through our observation, or at least that's how our brain has evolved to perceive the world. One extreme version of that is the Wheeler's Big 'U' universe where the universe is observing itself into existence. Find any resemblance to some of the origin myths? Not everybody agreed with this interpretation, which included Nobel laureates like Einstein and Schrödinger.

To show how bizarre Copenhagen interpretation was, Schrödinger proposed the famous quantum cat experiment. The paradox was conceived by Schrödinger in 1935, couple of years after he won the Nobel Prize. In this thought experiment, the unfortunate cat was placed inside a box with a flask of poison. The flask would be shattered by a falling hammer once the Geiger counter detects radioactivity. The box also had a radioactive source that had 50% probability of decaying per hour. So, after an hour, was Schrödinger's cat dead or alive? To Schrödinger and Einstein, the feline was either dead or alive when inside the box, or really pissed off. By opening the box and observing it we just came to know the truth that already existed. Our knowledge or ignorance does not change the reality. Or that was what we thought. What Niels Bohr and Werner Heisenberg's theory was claiming was not that the cat was either dead or alive, but rather it was both dead and alive at the same time. On opening the box, and observing, the 'alive' wave function and the 'dead' wave function collapsed into a single one. To Schrödinger, this was nonsense.

Schrödinger's damn cat may be just a thought experiment, but the theory has been proven by many experiments since the idea first came out. Monroe et al. (1996), as mentioned in their paper 'A "Schrödinger Cat" Superposition State of an Atom', was able to take a single trapped ion and place it in a superposition state of two positions at once. The real challenge, however, was to replicate this in a big system, like the cat. Friedman et al. (2000) and Wal et al. (2000) published their experiments proving Schrödinger's hypothesis at a larger scale by using millions of electrons. However, they were still individual particles stacked together. In 2018, a team of researchers from UK and Australia replicated this weird quantum behaviour using tiny drums that were visible to the naked eye. This drum could vibrate and stand still at the same time when hit by a 'drumstick', in this case a laser light. The results are still subjective, and the scientists are trying to improve their experiment. But this small drum is a big step towards exploring the quantum phenomena at macroscopic scale. If proven, the implication could mean that the moon exists at a particular place in the sky only when observed, and when it is not observed, it turns into a wave of probability. It's you observing it that makes all the difference.

The alternative explanation of the quantum world is the 'many-world' interpretation. This was suggested by Hugh Everett II, a student at Princeton who worked with Wheeler. In his version, one does not need to collapse the wave, instead all possible future universes exist. Each version of you in each universe remember only one version that is associated with that particular universe since you are entangled with that universe. Going back to Schrödinger's cat, in the Copenhagen version, the cat is both dead and alive until observed. In 'many-world' interpretation, there would be one unfortunate scientist who would find a dead cat on opening the box, while another version of the scientist will be happy to see that the kitty is still alive. The dead and alive world do not communicate between each other as both states are decoherent.

Our brain has evolved to make us believe in a simple story about the universe that is a lot more mysterious than we can contemplate. When all positive and negative energy comes together, all we get is nothing, like before the Big Bang. When a particle travels all possible paths with all possible velocities at the same time, the resultant velocity is zero. So, is it possible that when all possible parallel universes exist at the same time, there are no resultant universe at all? The resultant of all possible you is nothing. You are nothing! Reality as we know it is observer created. May be, the actual weirdness lies not in the world, but in the way we perceive it. We cannot sense more than 3 dimensions, we cannot see more than the VIBGYOR, we have a limited audible range, and even our sense of feeling is limited. The reality is as we perceive it through our flawed sense organs. And then the brain tries to make sense of that information, which is unique for each individual. There is no 'reality' outside that perception. So, has our brain been lying to us all along?

Unlearning the rainbow

It is hard to agree that things are not the way we observe them. In reality, most of what our brain constructs as facts are just stories we are served from our childhood. To appreciate it better, I asked four simple questions to my audience in one of my talks. I will ask the same to you. Do not think too much while answering them. Just answer what you feel. These are not brain twisters or puzzles, just simple questions that have simple answers.

Question 1: I held a white paper with a filled black circle in its centre and asked my colleagues what they saw.

Question 2: This was a no-brainer. How many colours are there in a rainbow?

Question 3: I had two world maps. One was the usual map with north on the top and other with south on the top. The question was, which side is up?

Question 4: This was the most difficult one and had to do with the viral dress colour problem that stormed the Internet in 2015. I asked them to name the two colours in the dress.

Now let us go back to the questions and try to find out how our brain works.

Question 1: 80% of the answers were 'black circle' or 'dot',which is of course correct.

But I also displayed a piece of paper. And that piece of paper had a white background. The white takes more space than the black. Just because it is white, it is not nothing. As a matter of fact, you do not actually see the circle. The circle is black, and no light is coming out of it. How can you see without light? The data you receive is that of the white background with no information from the centre circle. But what most of us 'see' is just the circle. Why? Because our brains are particularly good at finding anomalies. Anomalies could mean threats to our hunter and gatherer ancestors, and detecting them in advance helped us survive in the wild. Our brain does not always interpret all the things we see. It ignores the routine background and focuses on anomalies. Evolution wired us that way. Seeing isn't always the complete truth. That is why first impressions are mostly wrong, but we cannot stop making them.

Question 2: I asked how many colours are there in a rainbow. Almost unanimously everyone said 'seven'. Again, it is not incorrect. That is exactly what my daughter is taught at school. But have we ever asked ourselves why seven? Rainbows are made of continuous electromagnetic spectrum, and not discrete bands of seven colours. Rainbow has all the colours in the spectrum, and most human eye can distinguish almost 10 million different colours. Why seven then? Because we were told so. Indians and Greeks have been fascinated by the number seven. When you get obsessed with something, you see it everywhere. We are biased towards things we hold close. We have been so prejudiced that we made seven oceans, seven continents, seven heavens, seven days, seven sins, seven 'classical' planets and seven wonders. Even fiction prefers the magic number seven. Snow White met seven dwarfs, Sindbad the sailor had seven voyages, and then there is 007. We can as well make 6 or 20 oceans. We could have clubbed Europe and Asia into one continent. Why make Australia and Antarctica a new continent and leave out Greenland? Why limit it to just seven wonders and change the list every few years? Because modern world has been primed by number seven. Think about what other possible stories you have been primed with.

Question 3: Again, unanimously the map with north on top came out as the right answer.

This version of the map has been sold to us since our school days, and now we cannot think of an alternate possibility. Even Google maps have north on top by default. The earth is a sphere and both the maps are as incorrect as they are correct. Firstly, two-dimensional maps are a projection of a sphere in a plain paper and hence it is distorted. Leaving that apart, both maps are correct. Just because Europeans, who made this maps for the first time, were from the northern hemisphere, the north on top version became a norm. In fact 'up' is a direction opposite to gravity. We stand on the earth perpendicular to the ground. So the real up is away from the map. It is very local and the universe does not have an up direction. So, if you rotate the map and have South Pole as up, that is also a correct version. But then, no one taught us to question the obvious.

Question 4: This one is the most interesting. Most of us have seen this picture before as it became viral globally. If not, you can search 'The Dress' in Google. When asked what the colour of the dress was, one group of individuals saw blue and black while the other said white and golden. How is that possible? How can both be true? Our brain has this ability to interpret the colours not as we see, but as it thinks it should be. Our brain does not show us the actual colours. It tries to construct what it thinks is the true colour. So, it tries to remove filters, it removes the effect of sunlight and shadow, and other things that might affect the picture. It does a wonderful job of picture editing, by assuming the background and the brightness of the light. But, with the dress, our brain had a unique problem. A yellow filter on blue and blue filter on yellow shows the same colour. Which means, there were two different solutions to the colours of the dress, depending on your assumption of background and brightness. The picture is cropped in a way that there is no information about either. Our brain can have only one solution. So, it deduces it one way for one person, and other way for another. Looks are indeed deceptive. You might have noticed that the sun and moon appear larger near the horizon. This has puzzled human beings since the time they first saw it. Unfortunately, when you take a picture of the majestic celestial body, the size shrinks. This is called the 'Problem of Luna Mendex'. While there are many theories, no one really knows why the brain does it. But the brain somehow fools us and creates a rosy picture. It is not just the vision, even hearing is no different. This was evident from another viral post of 2018, this time an auditory clip, 'Yanny or Laurel'. About 53% people heard 'Laurel' and rest 'Yanny' on hearing the same audio clip. 'Yanny' can be heard at higher frequencies while 'Laurel' at lower frequencies. What you hear depends on how your ear-drums vibrate and how your brain deduces the vibrations. Each one of us perceive the world in a slightly different way. We all have our own unique world. Conflicts occur when we forget that there is more than one possible interpretation of the same information.

According to the National Science Foundation, our brains produce around 12,000 to 50,000 thoughts per day. Information travels inside the brain at a speed of up to 120 mps. Our brain is a very powerful organ, but it can easily get biased. It makes sense of the world by associating new information with memories which are often prejudiced and stereotyped. Our brain identifies anomalies and ignores the background, and it infers things in its own simple way, using mental shortcuts. This results in different types of heuristics and biases. It often does this to quickly come to a decision which is very important during an emergency. However, this gift of evolution, can also force us to take wrong decisions. One of the most common of such biases is anchoring. Anchoring affect happens when one gets influenced by irrelevant numbers. For example, I once asked a group of people to guesstimate the population of Cape

Town, and write it down on a piece of paper I provided. In half the paper, an arbitrary number of 10 million was written, while in another half 50,000. Even though the two numbers had no relevance, the former group came up with an average population number that was almost double of the latter group. Anchoring happened despite of telling them that the number on the paper was random and had no meaning. You often do not realize what thoughts you have anchored yourself to while making a decision.

Another common bias is the availability bias, where we tend to think that the possibilities that we can recall must have more importance than those we cannot. Many a times we can ignore the most likely outcome just because it is not easy to recall it. We have lazy brains. Quite similar to it is the confirmation bias, where we tend to seek out information that supports our pre-existing belief. Most of the political debates are anchored by confirmation bias. Such debates can get animated in no time. Some people tend to oppose new revolutionary ideas and stick with old tried and tested formulas. This is called the conservatism bias. Such preconception is what led to Galileo's house arrest. Then there is optimism bias, which happen when one undermines the risk and cost of a negative event because they ignore the known unknowns and are oblivious of the unknown unknowns. This often leads to taking up of risky projects that has high chance of failure. Affect heuristic occurs when we tend to take decision based on emotions. Depending on how a question is framed, one may underestimate or overestimate the impact of a situation because it struck a particular cord in their heart. For example, images of tragedy can make us overestimate the impact compared to numbers and stats. Over confidence effect is a well-established bias where one tends to be overconfident on one's decision and stick to it, despite reality showing otherwise. For example, when one has made a particular investment that he/she likes and the value of investment is falling, there is a tendency to hold on to it and keep making losses. It is also known as the sunk-cost fallacy. On the opposite end is the bandwagon effect where you tend to go with the crowd rather than your own decision. The crowd may be your entire nation, or just your small family. It is a kind of priming where you get influenced by the larger population while making a decision. This helps groups stay together and survive. This is the kind of bias that has made religion and nationalism so popular. What I mentioned here are just a few of the different types of biases.

While thinking about the future, we are influenced by our present state of mind. If we are happy, we predict a future event in a positive light than if we are sad. We like or dislike things based on comparisons which are often baseless. Most shoppers would rather buy a T-shirt whose price came down from INR1000 to INR 800, than the same quality T-shirt whose price went up from INR500 to INR 700. Using our irrationality, marketing guys have been fooling us for a long time to buy their preferred product despite giving us apparent choices by using the decoy effect. It is probably not possible to avoid all types of biases at all times, but it is important to keep them in mind while making important decisions, be it a professional or a personal one. From our childhood, we have been fed lies, like the rainbow has seven colours. As a child, we are innocent, and believe what is taught to us. When we grow up, we become egoistic. That ego prevents us from accepting that our childhood learnings might be wrong. So, we look for evidences to reinforce our stories. We also get busy with our lives, and have less time to question our subconscious prejudices. It is always a good idea to take a break from serious routine and give oneself the time to pause and ponder. If we want to make the right decisions in life, we need to be aware of these pitfalls and start unlearning the rainbow, one colour at a time.

The universe inside 1.2 kg protein

We take too many things for granted, like our senses and the time-space around us. You might have a perfect vision, but no sight; you might see the words, but not recognize the texts; you might hear, but not identify the rhythm of your favourite song. This happens to patients with the condition called agnosia. Since our reality is brain's interpretation, a small glitch in it's hardwire can significantly alter the reality. Even the reality of the space we live in. The memories and experiences stored in the brain makes no sense if there is no space. But where exactly does the 'space' reside? Injury to a particular part of the brain can make a person space-less. In one particular case, a person lost the sense of his left half of the world after a head injury. Such patients receive information, but cannot make sense of it because their brain fails to interpret the information. Then there are people who hear shapes, see noises and feel sounds! Ever heard of synesthesia? This unification of senses is quite astonishing considering the fact that there is no central control system in the brain. Each sense is controlled by different parts of the brain. What then unites all these senses? Is it conscience?

Our world and everything we perceive lies within the 1.2 kg mass of protein inside our skull. It consists of around 100 billion neurons that probably have no clue about who you are. Each one has its own bits of information that, like a puzzle, fit together to create us. There is no denying the fact that the brain is the most miraculous creation of evolution. In spite of the individual nerve cells, reacting to biochemical signals, having no idea about you, it helps you identify music from acoustic waves, words from random lines on papers, fall in love, cry, laugh and influence the world. It is a fascinating machine of which we don't know much. The irony is that we can only know and think about it, with it. When we say that humans have the most advanced brains, it is simply our brain bragging about itself. With that paradox in mind, let us understand what we know about how we perceive the universe through our five sense organs.

Vision is our strongest sense. About half the cortex in our brain is related to vision. That is why for humans, 'seeing is believing'. For dogs, it would be smelling is believing. For bats, hearing is believing. What is vision, after all? It is just billions of photons reflecting from an object and hitting the rods and cones within your eyes, and the brain then creating an image of that information. Our rods and cones are programmed in a way that they get excited by just one percent of the electromagnetic spectrum. You are not seeing the object; you are seeing only the photons that hit the right spots in your eyes. Those photons display wave-particle dual behaviour and follow the laws of Quantum Mechanics. Is it possible that our brain is wired to comprehend information in the classical sense and hence it is very difficult to observe the quantum world on a large scale?

While we are indirectly 'seeing' the world, it is doing a fine job of helping us survive. The whole process of 'seeing' is very complicated and is lucidly explained in the book *Cognitive Psychology* by Oxford Publication. When the photons coming from the object in sight passes through the cornea of your eye, it goes into the anterior chamber, and then through a specialized lens into the major chamber which is filled with a fluid called vitreous humour. The lens and cornea evolved in a way to focus the photons exactly into the retina. The receptor cells in the retina fire neurons once the photons hit it. You can now appreciate how complex the whole process is. It amazes me how, by random mutation and natural selection, evolution managed to create this sophisticated machine. Things start getting more complicated from there on. The receptor cells are of two types – rods and cones (named according to their shape). Rods are better at helping us see at night. Cones reveal the finer details and help us differentiate between different wavelengths of the photons hitting it, and thus interpret colours. Colours are not reality. We casually say that light has three primary colours. That's absolutely wrong. Primary colours are not a property of light, but our eyes. The colours are primary because there are three sets of cones in our eyes. One set is most sensitive to the red wavelength, another to green light and the third to the blue.

There are few women who have four types of cones and a much more colourful world. Our cones can even sense part of ultra-violet spectrum once the lenses in our eyes are removed. The eye lenses filter ultraviolet rays to protect the eye. People in whom the lens had to be operationally removed, see the world in different colours.

The nocturnal animals have more rods than photons to help them see better in the dark. These receptor cells send the information about the photons to the brain via retinal ganglion cells. If you gently press the corner of your closed eyes just next to your nose, you will see a small spot of light. The pressing causes your retina to bend, which creates the same signal as that when the photons hit the retina. Once there is a signal, photon or not, the brain will infer it as light. Ganglion cells connect the eye to the brain and it starts from the blind spot of our eye. The blind spot has no rods and cones as the area is already occupied by blood vessels and nerve axions. Ganglion connects to the brain in an area known as visual cortex. Two separate interpretation chambers process the information brought from the eye – the ventral and dorsal stream (David Milner and Melvyn A. Goodale, 1992). The ventral stream ('what' pathway) deals with understanding patterns and recognition of objects. The dorsal stream ('where' pathway) helps identify position and movement of objects. It receives information faster, helping us avoid potential dangers. The two systems are very much interconnected.

Accurate recognition of objects requires information from both eyes, preferably photons coming from different angles (as object or the observer moves relative to each other), and information stored in the memory to compare. The image in the retina is two-dimensional, but the brain somehow processes two two-dimensional images from both eyes and creates a pretty accurate three-dimensional image. Without it, we would never be able to gauze distance, and hence speed. So, the depth of space as we see it, is our brain's construct.

We take the spatial information for granted without often appreciating the fact that reality is more complicated. Brain damage, especially in the right hemisphere, can result in sensory neglect where objects on a particular side of the patient can go completely unnoticed. Driver and Halligan demonstrated in 1991 that such neglect is associated with object rather than the scene. Instead of ignoring, say the entire left view, the patient will ignore the left half of all objects. If you play chess with such patients, they will move pieces from only one side of the board, as if the other half does not exist. If you tell them to describe an object from memory, they will talk in detail about only one half of it. Now, if you change their orientation and tell them to remember the same object, but from the other side, they will tell you details of the previously neglected part. This time, completely neglecting the previous part they described. While the memories were intact, the conscious information depended on the spatial reference. A more extreme form of such case is called Balint's syndrome, where the patient loses the ability to sense the visual field as a whole. They perceive the world as a series of single objects, rather than the entire picture. For example, if their attention is focused on the glasses on your face, they will not be able to see your face. The brain's entire focus will be on any one specific object. In fact, single objects are how we see the world too. What separates us from the patients with Balint's syndrome is our ability to quickly shift focus from one object to another. In Balint's syndrome, the patient loses the ability to shift focus.

The process of object recognition is entirely different from the process of face recognition. Studies showed that the problem faced by those having damage in one particular part of the brain is either to do with face recognition, or object recognition, and never both. Face recognition, involves not just identifying familiar from non-familiar faces, but also understanding that it is an actual human face and not a doll, the emotions that the face is showing, the sex of the person, attractiveness, and even ethnicity. We can easily recognize the 20-year-old picture of our partner when we see it for the first time, even though we never met during childhood. No one fully understands how exactly the brain manages to do it. It is probably a mixture of resemblance match, analogs and a bit of reconstruction. The whole process of seeing and recognizing is not as simple as it seems. Our brain performs processing of vast data to make life simple for us. The photons act as proxy of the object, and our brain interprets the image of that object from the limited information it has. It is like 'seeing' the wall, blindfolded, just by throwing and catching balls reflected from it. All you know is how hard the ball hits your palm. You make an entire image out of that proxy information.

While visual recognition is quicker and more accurate for distance objects, touching aids one acquire additional information like texture, temperature, pressure (weight), along with love, care and pleasure. But you are not truly touching anything. When you are sitting on a chair, you are not really sitting on it; you are floating in the air, an infinitesimally small distance above the chair. The electrons in the chair are continuously repelling the electrons in your body as you float. That repulsion is the reason why you cannot pass through the wall. Thanks to the electrons, else I would have never been able to sit on a commode! Think about this, when you are kissing your partner you are not really touching his/her lips. Thanks again to the electrons; else you would have passed right through. What an embarrassment that would have been. Please do not think of this while you are kissing. It will be an unnecessary distraction that can significantly reduce the chance of spreading your genes.

Feeling of touch is just the invisible repulsive force of the electrons. The nerve is passing that information to the brain, which in turn is interpreting it as hot, cold, pleasure or pain. Experiments have shown that by activating different parts of your brain, you can have a false sense of feeling. But what is more intriguing is how the brain manages to pinpoint the exact location of objects we are about to touch. Closing your eyes and touching your nose is a very complicated process made simple by our brains. Knowing precise position of our finger is a skill we learn over time. Toddlers cannot do that. The brain has to deduce the location of the fingers with respect to the hand, and hands with respect to the arm, and the arms with respect to the body. This process that helps us sense the relative position of our body parts even has a name, and is called proprioception. The procedure of perceiving the body movements is called kinesthesia. 'Rubber hand illusion' performed by Italian researchers revealed how the brain recognizes our body. In this experiment, a fake rubber hand was placed in front of the subjects and the real hand was hidden out of sight. Both the real and fake hands were then stroked in the same way at exactly the same place for a minute or two. The brain slowly started to consider the fake hand as its own and disowned the real hand. The subject reacted when the fake hand was pinched, as if it was his own. We talked about how the brain paints an image based on the information from our senses. What is more intruding is the fact that parts of that image are the brain's own creation and nothing to do with the actual information.

Hearing, we all know, can be the most deceptive of all senses, unless you are a bat. Just like colours, there is nothing as sound outside your brain. It is not only an empty world, but also a quiet one. Sound is just the interpretation of the vibrations of your eardrums. And that again is limited to the frequencies of 20 to 20,000 Hz. How much can you depend on that thin tympanic membrane? Quite a lot, actually. Hearing is almost as complicated as seeing. While you can turn your eyes away from things you don't like to see, it is almost impossible to turn away from a specific sound that you do not want to hear without blocking all sounds. But, somehow, even in a busy place like the Kolkata Coffee Shop where hundreds of people are talking at the same time, you can easily have a conversation with your friends, completely ignoring the rest of the noise. In the same place, if a new friend joins you and calls your name from another end of the room, it promptly catches your attention. Not just that, you can pretty accurately locate the corner from where your friend is calling. How is your brain doing that with just vibrations of little ear drums at its disposal? Let's just say that your brain is damn smart. There are two things happening here. First, your brain is processing all the data and helping you focus your attention on what you want. The second is locating the source of the sound. Your brain processes all the information from your eardrums in parallel and then selects the ones you are attentive towards. The rest is not in your conscious brain and is probably erased after a period of time. However, experiments have shown that we are unconsciously aware, and often get affected, by the noise that we are not attentive to. When happy words are played in the ears of participants at such a fast rate that they cannot identify the words, they still became happier after words were played. Same thing happens with negative emotions. Our brain registers more information than it makes us conscious of. In one particular experiment, words related to old age were played in the ears of the subjects. Even though the words did not get consciously registered in the brain of the participants, the movement of the subjects slowed down after the experiment. This experiment demonstrated that we can get influenced by things that we are not aware of. The environment or community we live in can sub-consciously mould us.

Locating sound in three-dimensions is more complicated than just identifying. Both ears hear the same noise, but owing to their different location in the head, the signal in each ear is slightly different. This slight difference in the timing and intensity of the vibration of your eardrums in both your ears is enough to locate the sound. The ear that is further from the sound gets shadowed by the head and receives lower intensity sound, provided the wavelength of the sound is smaller than the head. The brain can process that tiny difference to locate the source of the sound. What happens when the wavelength of the sound is longer than the distance between the ears? Then the wave passes without even noticing the head. In the latter case, the time lag between the two ears comes to rescue. Since the wavelength is larger than the head size, there is a point in time when both ears are within the wavelength, but at different locations in the wave. The brain can identify that and use that information to locate the sound. This technique does not work for smaller wavelengths, as the ear cannot identify a particular wave unless it is long enough to pass through both the ears at the same time. Both these methods complement each other very well. Trouble arises in rare occasions when the wavelength of the sound is of the same size as the distance between the two ears. Then it becomes impossible to locate the sound. There are animals that use this flaw to communicate with others without revealing their location to the predators.

Do you know that apples, onions and potatoes taste the same? It's the smell that makes all the difference. Yes, taste and smell are very much related. You can't really depend on your taste buds with a blocked nose, can you? Taste buds are the receptors of taste and are mostly located in the tongue. There are few in the roof of the mouth and the pharynx. The taste buds are specialized to identify different chemicals and pass on the information about the chemicals as different tastes. The five basic tastes are salty, sweet, sour, bitter and umami (savoury). There are no taste buds for spicy hot. In fact, the so-called taste of the chilies is in fact allergies that trigger the same receptors of the skin that respond to heat. No wonder we call it hot. Smell, like taste, also responds to chemicals. The nose cavity has the olfactory (smell) receptors inside the mucous membrane, also called olfactory epithelium. Human beings have around 400 functional odor receptor genes that help us smell the world. There is also an auxiliary olfactory sense organ called vomeronasal organ that specializes in detecting pheromones. Pheromones are secreted in underarms and using deodorants might suppress its effect. Experiments have shown that both men and women under influence of pheromones rate all men or women of opposite sex as more attractive. So, if you really want to attract someone, ditch the deodorant.

Our senses are only doing remote sensing. It is doing a good job, but the interpretation of the assumed reality is a gross oversimplification. We are not programmed to sense all types of information that exists (like magnetic field), and even the information that we can perceive is limited. Human ears can hear only 20-20,000 Hz of acoustic wavelength and see just 400-700 nm of electromagnetic spectrum. Even the sense of touch has its limit. We do not sense a mosquito sitting on our skin, at least not until it starts sucking our blood. We can neither smell nor taste all chemicals. Most of us assume that the world is as we understand it, and others (including other animals) would take it in the same way. But that is not the case. We all have our own universes inside our 1.2 kg brains. Our brains order information in a definite pattern to make meaning out of it. What we perceive is that meaning, to each his/her own.

How do we make sense of the universe around us?

In this age of information, we are constantly being bombarded with data that affect our perception. Often times, the media persistently project a single story that gets imprinted in our brains, leading to prejudice. A country like India can be thought of as very unsafe for women. US could be thought of as a precarious place where you might get shot down the moment you land. People from Nigeria might be considered as tribal, even though Nigeria has perfectly modern cities. Once we are anchored to a particular way of thinking, it becomes very difficult to get rid of the prejudices. We often fail to comprehend that our opinion might be just one of the thousand possible stories that we have never heard. The single stories themselves may not be wrong. But, it is just a one-sided story. Truth is multi-faceted.

Is our future multi-faceted too? Or is it that we do not have any free will?

Scott Adam's 2004 Dilbert cartoon aptly says, 'Free will is an illusion. People always choose the perceived path of greatest pleasure.' Do we have free will? One would have thought that science has already solved this problem. Quite surprisingly, it hasn't. It has only changed the way we look at the question. No more do we think that we are at the mercy of some higher powers. The problem of free will is not about the lack of choice or determinism, but about the way we choose. We may like to think that we are in control of our life, at least till we get married! Unfortunately, most of the things that happen to us are outside our control. I did not choose when, where and to whom I was born. I did not select my genes. And in all likelihood, I will have no free will about my death. My looks, my gender, my religion and nationality were predetermined. However, all these factors had a strong influence in determining who I am today. My genetics determines my nature, and my family determines my nurture. This means that we can never have complete freedom of choice. Random events along with our nature and nurture limit the choices we have. Having said that, there are a lot of things that are within our sphere of influence, like the way I want to colour my hair, the profession I want to be in, choosing my partner or when to have a baby. Even the choices that are in our control are influenced by external factors, especially our family. Rich people will have a different set of options than poor people for the same problem. Often our parents and teachers influence our career and thus the profession we choose. Choosing your partner is not just a one-sided decision; the other person needs to agree as well. When to have a baby, and sometimes even what colour you want your hair to be, is often a decision that you make along with your partner. How much of free will does that leave us with?

Let us ignore all the external factors for the time being and say that only you decide what to choose. When I started having thyroid problems, I noticed that I lost my temper very easily. I became a different person. It made me realize that a lot of what we are depends on the biochemical that flow in our body. These, in turn, depend on our brain. This is well documented in the case of Phineas P. Gage. In 1848, Gage suffered a major accident and lost a part of his brain. The loss of that particular part of the brain, prefrontal lobe to be exact, turned a cheerful well-mannered gentleman into a self-destructive habitual liar. Similar cases have been observed with other individuals with damaged prefrontal lobe. The prefrontal lobe, we now know, controls our emotions. Recent studies in neuroscience indicate that our thoughts could well be a product of biochemical algorithms written in our brain.

How we behave and react to situations depend more on the structure of our brain rather than the situation itself. Take for example the feelings of fear, anger, lust and love. They are the same all around the globe because they stem from the genetic make-up of our species and those feelings results from secretion of same biochemicals. When we are threatened, our brain releases adrenalin and cortisol that create the feeling of fear. Lust is governed by dopamine while the feeling of love by oxytocin. These chemicals are not any different for an African or a Chinese or a European. These chemicals can even be released artificially by intake of drugs or stimulating the right part of the brain through electrodes. We will have the feeling, corresponding to the part that is triggered, without any reason for feeling the same. What if the choice you are about to make is guided by your brain's chemistry, determined by your genes and memories that you have no control over, following all the rules of physics that are fixed? We are a very negligible part of the entire universe. If the laws of physics guide everything in the universe, including the birth of the galaxy and origin of life, then why would our thoughts, or we for that matter, be any different?

This begs the question, where is free will? An interesting experiment was done almost 35 years ago by Dr. Benjamin Libet. Libet's Experiment demonstrated that the unconscious response precedes, and potentially cause conscious or volitional decisions 300 milliseconds before you actually take that decision! If our unconscious mind is deciding for us, then it puts some serious doubts on our free will. Are we mistaking randomness for free will? The experiment received widespread fame and critics. May be our conscious mind has a veto power. May be, the way the experiment was conducted had flaws. Even then, we cannot disagree about the fact that absolute free will is a myth.

A 40-year-old man became addicted to child pornography after he developed tumour in the or bitofrontal cortex. Once the tumour was removed, his addiction vanished. Similarly, Charles Whitman, a 25-year-old loving husband suddenly turned into a mass murderer. The cause was a large tumour that pressed down his amygdala, a part of the brain that controls emotion. This brings us to the dilemma of justice. Who do we blame in such situation, the person or the tumour? Every decision we take is in some way affected by our genes, the way we were brought up, and any changes or damages that may happen to our brain. Some might argue that it is the non-conscious process in the brain that drives all our actions. While we can never be completely free, I would like to believe that we are not completely helpless about deciding our future. Or, at least my brain would want me to believe that. While the biochemical inside our body affect our behaviour, our behaviour in turn can affect the chemicals. With help of the right lifestyle, we can change the way we behave. With the help of medical treatments we can cure thyroid problems or tumours. I sincerely hope that it is not the apparent chaos which gives us the illusion of free will.

The way we make sense of the world depends on the way our brain receives information coming through the sense organs and make stories. In truth, we cannot sense anything directly. All our perceptions are indirect, with the help of proxies. We can go to the extent of saying that our perception is more of a hallucination than reality. One might say that our sense organs do a pretty good job of replicating the reality in our minds. That is why my interpretation of the world broadly matches yours. The Taj Mahal is the same for all the people who have seen it. Its beauty might be just in our brain, but the physical reality of the Taj Mahal has to exist. There must be a fundamental reality that is beyond the boundaries of our mind. What if we all are biased in the same way? We have evolved together and almost have the same genes. Since our brain is similar, our understanding has to be similar. Then there are a lot of things that we assume should match, actually does not. Different people interpret the same thing in different ways. Some may observe details, while others see the big picture. Some people have brains focused on facts, while others may be more imaginative. There is no right or wrong way to make sense of the universe. Even fundamental things like time and space are more mysterious than we think. Experiments in quantum physics are destroying the very fabric of our known comfortable world. And, it is not just at the micro scale. New experiments are replicating the weirdness of quantum world in macro scale. All possible realities might exist, and we just happen to remember one at a time. May be in one of the universes it is Schrödinger who is in the box and is both dead and alive till Dr. Cat opens it. The single universe of Classical Physics might be the simplified story that our brain writes. Keeping that in mind is very important as we move into the next chapter.

There is still a huge gap in our understanding about how we make sense of the universe and how consciousness works. A fascinating study recently published in PNAS journal shows how giant neurons deep within our brainstem, called Nucleus gigan to cellularis or black box, might stimulate consciousness, awareness and cognition. There is a reason it is called black box. We know very little about it. Maybe, once we know exactly how we convert the chemical signals from our imperfect sense organs into consciousness, we would know what it means to be human beings. To learn about the truth, we need to start unlearning our prejudices. Once we start to question our deep-rooted faith, we will see that the gap between the good and the bad starts to fade. Even a lot of our moral values become irrelevant.

Question 3

Is Sex Bad?

'Sex lies at the root of life, and we can never learn to reverence life until we know how to understand sex.'

– Havelock Ellis, *Studies in the Psychology of Sex* (1897)

Gender blender

I can see your eyes lit up the moment you saw the word 'sex'. This three letter word attracts people like fire attracts flies. Sex is one of the most loved word and at the same time the most hated. Before we try to appreciate this irony, let us dwell with the less attractive meaning of the word. Ever wondered what would have happened to Marlin, father of Nemo, once his beloved wife died, if the story was not conceived by the biased opinion of the human mind? He would not have stayed Marlin, but become Marla. Marlin and Nemo belong to a strange species called clown-fish, who are sequential hermaphrodites. Which means that they have the freedom of changing their sex without the need of costly, far from perfect, surgeries. Once the female dies, the largest male undergoes a sex change and takes her position. Marlin's position, in turn, would be taken up by the non-mating males in the group. I was surprised when I first heard that. Sex, in my mind, was something fixed. There were only two types of sexes, governed by genes. Apparently, my idea about sex was completely wrong. In some reptiles and fishes, the temperature of the egg or size of the organism related to its competitors determines sex. While in *Homo sapiens* the presence of the Y chromosome determines sex, in birds, reptiles and some insects, it is reversed. In them, it is the females that carry two different chromosomes. The boundaries of sex aren't always sharp. It may sound impossible, but gender and sex are more fluid than what most human mind can comprehend. That's the reason we have taboo associated with sex (and even gender) that does not fit our mindset.

For human beings, a person having XY chromosome is usually a male, and one having YY chromosome is a female. Or that is what we have been told in our biology classes. Nobody told us that it was not the rule. A person with XY chromosome (genetically male) can still develop female genitals if the SRY (Sex Determining Region Y) protein in the gene on Y-chromosome is inactive. Such a person would be no different from any other female. This is just one example. There are numerous individuals who do not fit the artificial binary classification because nature is more versatile than our mind. There are people in whom the ovary or testis never develop. There are males having sex chromosome pattern of XXY instead of XY. Similarly, there are females whose chromosome pattern is XO instead of XX. There are persons in the world whose genetic sex is XY and the gonads are exclusively testes, but the external genitalia are either ambiguous or completely female or vice versa. These people are not anomalies as many would like you to believe, but part of the natural variation of genes that keeps the diversity alive and helps us evolve.

While sex is biological and determined by one's reproductive system, gender is more socio-cultural and determined by one's preference or role one plays crudely based on his or her sex. Gender determination is more complicated then sex, especially because often a person does not realize her/his gender till she/he has grown old enough. Our ancestors recognized and respected the complexity of human gender. Genders other than male and female finds place in ancient mythologies of both East (*Ardhanarishvara*) and West (*Aphroditus*). *Triteeyaprakrti*, or the third sex, is mentioned in Hindu texts as old as 2nd century BC. In many places around the world, we still find the customs of trans-sexuals like Samoan *fa'afafine*, Indian *Hijra*, *Kathoeys* of Malaysia and 'Two-Spirits' of Native America. However, their status has gone down drastically over the years, and now they have to struggle to find a proper job and a proper life. This happened because contemporary stories are making our mind more rigid and binary. We grow up hearing stories of good vs bad, right vs wrong, rich vs poor, right vs left, etc. Even the fairy tales have heroes and demons. Unknowingly, we are getting trained for a polarized view of the world. Add to that the Victorian orthodoxy that spread after the industrial revolution. Now we find it difficult to place the alternate genders in the strict binary classification schemes, making these perfectly natural human beings an apparent 'anomaly'. The polarized view imparted by culture coupled with our genetic adverse reaction to 'anomalies' gives rise to bigotry. The so-called 'anomaly' might be as high as

10% of world population. We will be missing all the productive work they can do to make our planet a better place if they struggle to join the mainstream because of our silly prejudices.

Some cultures around the world recognize more than six genders, which might seem absurd to the modern mind. Let's try to look at the spectrum of gender to appreciate it further. This is not a classification, but just shows the wide gamut:

Masculine Male: People with male bodies who prefer females
Feminine Female: People with female bodies who prefer males
Lesbian: People with female bodies who prefer females
Gay: People with male bodies who prefer males
Bisexual: People who like both male and female partners
Transgender: People who consider themselves neither male nor female

There are people who are forced by society to behave like a gender that they were not born in, like the Eunuchs or the Sworn Virgins of Albania. Since traditional laws of Albania permit only male members of the family to own the property, some females follow the practice of sworn virginhood and live like males to keep owning the property. The women take oath in front of the village elders and then she is permitted by law to live as a man. A sworn virgin would dress like a man, use a male name, carry a gun, smoke, drink, work, sing and dance, just like the men.

Gender can itself be genetic and separate from genitals. It has been found that a specific region of the chromosome, that biologists gave a boring name XQ-28, determines the sexual orientation of males. XQ-28 is possibly attached to the X-chromosome, and thus transferred from the maternal side. In fact, there is no one single gene that determines sexual orientation. There is a particular gene in chromosome 13 called SLITRK6, which is very active in diencephalon (a part of our brain), that influences sexual orientation in boys and men. There is also evidence of TSHR in chromosome-14, which mainly control thyroid activity, to affect sexual preference. Research on linking lesbian preference to genes is lagging behind as women are more complicated (rather fluid) in their preference. A recent study at University of Lie'ge by Julie Bakker showed that brain activator pattern of young transgender people (both boys and girls) were similar to their experience gender than their sex at birth. Even the regional gray matter and white matter volumes of the brain matched their preferred gender.

It is time society realizes that gender is not just a lifestyle choice, but an innate nature. A strict binary gender classification puts immense stress on persons who cannot place themselves into either of the two categories. Even a third category isn't enough. Such categorization results in people trying to force fit themselves into one of the established categories. Many of them are left with no options, but to go under the knife and change their sex to something more acceptable to the world. In that process, many lose their own identity and spend the rest of their life under immense mental trauma. It often results in suicides. This trauma can also become physical. It is seen that 76 countries around the world still consider homosexuality illegal, with five of them having death penalties as punishment. In countries where it is legal, many still make fun of them and they are stereotyped as comedians, even in movies. May be it is time to read fairy tale books to our children where all possible gender relations are present. Until and unless we find a way to erase the taboos of gender from our mind, a large chunk of our population will remain without justice, left to suffer in silence in the dark corners of our society.

Female fatale

If you open any men's magazine, it will be full of pictures of naked or half-dressed women. It turns men on. So what do all the women's magazine feature? Again naked or half-dressed women! Most of us will agree that female *Homo sapiens* are beautiful, unlike the males. Human beings seem to be the only species where females are more beautiful than the lumpy and furry male counterparts... or may be beauty just lies in the eyes of the beholder! However, it is surprising that it is the women who are more conscious about their looks. When men wake up in the morning, they are as good looking as when they went to bed. Women, however, deteriorate during the night. Only in their mind, of course. Not only do we look different, our thought processes are different too. Men's brains are solution-oriented and woman's brains are process-oriented. Men can think of only one thing at a time, while women are good at multi-tasking. Women will lie to make you feel good while most men will lie to make themselves look good. When we talk of gender equality, we must remember that equality is not about being same, because we are programmed a bit differently.

Women are often the hidden half of history, while men have dominated the public arena. Since antiquity, women have silently left their mark on the world, and at times have changed it. Not many people know that it was a Chinese empress named Xilingshi who invented sericulture around 3000BC that made China a world power; the first known author in the world was a lady named En Hedu'anna, a high priestess of Moon God in Ur who lived around 2300BC; there was an entire kingdom in Northern India, called '*Strirajya*', that was ruled by women for over thousand years as per many ancient texts; the world's first computer programmer, Ada, was a girl. Before the beginning of agriculture, in the stone-age, women were not just food gatherers, but also huntresses. These Eves were not only giving company to their Adams, but also doing much more. There are stone-age paintings preserved in Kashmir that show women going together with men for hunting. They also danced together to the beats of the ancient drums. These huntresses of the lithic era shared equal status with men. The first god human beings worshiped was the Great Mother. Among the first human images discovered are the Venus figures that date back to the Upper Paleolithic period between 35,000 and 10,000 BC. We can still feel the echoes of the beats in which these free women danced, when we see the cave paintings in Bhimbetka (Madhya Pradesh, India). The world has changed a lot since then. The number of condoms brought by unmarried women has increased six-fold in the last decade in India. This might give an apparent impression of sexual liberation. However, a culture that once celebrated sex and produced *Kamasutra*, the treatise on sex, is struggling for sexual liberation. Kisses are being censored from movies, posters are being removed because government thinks it is too revealing, and even condom advertisements are being banned from being shown during prime time shows. Let us take a quick look at how history has changed the status of the fairer sex.

The earliest evidence of *Homo sapiens* dates back to 300,000 years ago. For most part of our life, we lived as hunters and gatherers. Even today, there are some isolated tribes that live like our ancestors. The Negrito race of Andaman is one such race that has remained largely unchanged since the great coastal migration that happened around 70,000 years ago. They live in the forest and depend on hunting, fishing, and gathering. The tribal people still use primitive bows, arrows, and spears to hunt. They love pig meat, but hate birds or deer. These people hardly wear any clothes, but are fascinated about their ornaments. They are the last of the people who still live like the firsts. Most importantly, their idea of marriage and sex is much more fluid than ours. Divorces and widow marriages are very common. While there might be rules about choosing mates, premarital sex is neither uncommon, nor unsocial. However, something very basic changed with agriculture – possession.

Hunters and gatherers did not possess anything of real value, apart from some stone tools and clothes, which were easily replaceable. Agriculture ensured that you have more food than you need for a day. For the first time, you could store something of immense value for the future. Depending on the soil of the area you settled in and the skill sets, your tribe could be rich. Others without access to such fertile lands might not be that lucky. That was the beginning of income inequality, starting a war for wealth. Wealthy tribes needed to protect their wealth from other tribes. Men, the hunters, had distinctive advantage when it came to fighting. Hence the men became the protector of the new found wealth, and thus the possessor of the same. This also marks the beginning of patriarchy. We now know that there were female hunters too, and pre-historic women were much stronger on average than modern women. The past was quite different than the present. There were some societies that remained matriarchal, despite agriculture. So why does patriarchy dominate the modern world?

In the cradle of civilization, the Eurasian societies including the Indo-Aryans, Persians, Chinese, Greeks, Romans, Arabs, Turks, and Russians, were the first to become patriarchal. Some research points out that this was an influence of Kurgan culture which spread from Pontic Steppe north of the Black Sea to the rest of Eurasia. Matrilineal patterns are preferred in stable and peaceful societies. According to researchers Sanday (1981), Martin and Voorhies (1975), patriarchy is common in societies where endemic warfare is frequent and resources are scarce or where populations have been conquered by invading patrilineal tribes. The Kurgan tribes were aggressive and loved warfare. Their natural tendency was to become patriarchal. As they spread, they influenced the tribes they invaded. That's how Eurasia got its culture, and the modern world is dominated by Eurasian cultural influence, thanks to colonization. So, even some of the matrilineal tribes became slightly patrilineal over the years. Interestingly, some parts of Northeast (e.g. Khasi people) and South India (e.g. Marumakkathayam system of Kerala) that has been less influenced by the invasions starting from the Iranians, Greeks, Sakas Kushans to the Afghans, Moguls and Europeans, remains matrilineal.

Once you possess a lot of wealth, you would want to pass them to your children after you die. Our genes wanted to be sure that the advantage of survival was not lost down the line. Thus, men went to extremes in order to ensure that their wife only bore their child, to whom the wealth would go. While men continued to be polygamous, most societies ensured that women were monogamous. In some places, the female body was fully covered to protect them from gaze of other males, while other tribes mutilated the external female genitalia to decrease their libido to ensure their faithfulness. Women were forced to sacrifice their pleasure to protect men's wealth. This was a result of the change from the mobile hunter and gatherer narrative to that of sedentary agriculture based civilization.

In men's writings of the medieval age, women were carnal and lustful beings while men were spiritual. Quite a shift from the era of Mother Goddess. After all, in this new narrative they descended from Eve, the one who could not control her lust! Aristotle (384-322BC) believed that man is by nature superior to the female and so the man should rule and the woman should be ruled. Thomas Aquinas (1225-74) dismissed women as 'defective and misbegotten'. The laws of Manu states,'women, Sudra, dog and crow embody untruth, sin and darkness'. Creation stories also tell us a great deal about a society's view of women. In the

Judao-Christian version, Eve is the cause of all human misery. In fact, the first woman created by god was not Eve, but Lilith. Lilith and Adam were created together. Lilith dared to be independent and challenged Adam's superiority. Why should there be difference when both of them were created equal? That was not a valid argument at that time. Instead of making her equal, she was forced to become evil for the 'horrendous crime' of claiming equality. Free women were a threat to medieval men. In Greek mythology, the first woman, Pandora, was created as a form of punishment because men had learned from Prometheus the secret of making fire. Pandora was beautiful and irresistible to men, but she was made deliberately in a way that brought sorrow, harm and trouble to man. Such stories may seem unfair today, but in those bygone eras, this was the social norm.

The term 'husband' comes from Old Norse *hūsbōndi*, meaning 'house bound'. It is not much different from housewife. In modern world, the division of household work is much sharper than it was in the past. In fact, it was only during the Industrial Revolution that men were dragged out of the house and forced to work in factories. Now, such a division has become a rule. Interestingly, with the advancement of science due to industrial revolution, women slowly began to get back a bit of their lost status. But they had to fight for it. A group of men started the feminist revolution and later the women took over. The first wave of the feminist movement happened during 18th century, through to the early 20th century. It dealt mainly with the women's right to vote. Writers such as Virginia Woolf have left their influence with powerful writings during this wave. On 8 March 1917, Russian women led a revolution that overthrew the imperial government. The date was later chosen to mark International Women's Day. The second-wave (1960s-1980s) of feminism was largely concerned with issues of equality, such as the end to gender discrimination. The biggest myth of second wave was the whole bra-burning legend, a fable promoted by the media. The second-wave could not replicate the success of the first. The third wave of feminism (1990s-current) was about responding to the failures of the second wave, and had a greater focus on developing the different achievements of women. It was more subtle and more effective. These feminist movements helped women realize their value in the society and brought them back to recognition. With the advent of social media, there is a new spark in the feminist movement. From blackening of profile pictures to the #metoo campaign, feminism is spreading fast.

Success of this movement is very important. A survey conducted in 1996 showed that in both developed and developing countries, women worked 35 hours more than men every week. They feed families, carry water, collect fuel, and do the housework, but still these are not counted as work. About 90% of the rural female labour force have been labelled 'housewives'. Though women produce approximately 80% of the food on the planet, they receive less than 10% of agricultural assistance. In India itself, 18,233 brides were murdered or committed suicide because their marriage dowries were considered inadequate, in a statistics from 2012. Female infanticide is still common in many backward areas. History shows the hypocrisy of our society that downgrades that part of it without which it would not exist.

One has to be very careful not to lose focus from the key

issues, else the movement could fizz out like the second wave. Feminism is not a fight against men, but against a mindset that in prevalent in both men and women. Feminism is not about being equal. It is about having the equal opportunity to live a life of one's choice. In few of the developed cities, one can probably say that women have equal opportunity like men, however in most corners of the world, they are still fighting to get back their lost status. Even in the developed nations of our modern world, the male-female ratio of corporate offices is heavily skewed towards men. Pay gap between men and women exists everywhere. While the gap has reduced for early career men and women, there is still a substantial gap post pregnancy. It is a proven fact that being a parent hurt women's career substantially more than men's. This is technically termed as the 'child penalty'. Recent research suggests that child penalty suffered by women does not depend on husband or in-laws, but on the example set by their own mother. Working mothers have working daughters whose income reduction post childbirth is smaller because they compromise less on their careers.

While feminism is giving women more social power, latest studies indicate that women are better than men at surviving. Women's legs are not just sexy, but also supposed to be 5.8% stronger than men, and women are way ahead of men in terms of their immune system. XX chromosome makes women healthier because even in case of coding error in one X chromosome, there is a backup X chromosome. Men, on the other hand, have no such backups. Hence, any defect in their chromosomes will lead to disease more frequently. Emotionally as well, women are much better at dealing with trauma, heart disease or any other stress compared to men. One thing they are not good at, however, is taking risks. Research has pointed out that most women take less risk than men in both personal and professional life. Reshma Saujani, an education activist, explains in her Ted Talk how the difference in the way we bring up our boys verses our girls creates that difference. Girls are protected more than boys by their parents from the infancy. The 'lovely' and 'cute' daughters are mollycoddled at home. Even the classic children stories stereotype women. The princess and their entire life revolve around finding the one handsome prince. Once found, they live happily ever after. If we want women to make progress, we need to change this narrative. We need to break the stereotypes that unknowingly drags women back. It is time we let girls take risks, because girls who had learned to take risk in life have made wonders as women.

Razia Sultana became the only woman monarch to have ever ruled Delhi. The Gond queen Durgavati successfully ruled for fifteen years, before she lost her life in a battle with the Mughal emperor Akbar's general Asaf Khan in 1564. 'A'ishah, widow of Muhammad, rebelled against the Caliph Ali in the Battle of the Camel at Basra around 659 AD. In 1429, Joan of Arc, supported by Queen Yolande, began her military and religious campaign against the English. At the Battle of Orléans, she led the French army to victory. In 1553, Mary Tudor became the Queen of England. Her persecution of Protestants earned her the name Bloody Mary. Elizabeth I, half-sister of Mary Tudor, became Queen of England five years later. Rani Laxmibai, the Queen of Jhansi, valiantly fought against the British soldiers. Marie Curie broke the norm and became the first woman to win Noble Prize despite the struggles in her early life. There are numerous such examples. Women have always affected the business of everyday life. As mothers they raised families, as lovers they gave meaning to life, as daughters they took care of their parents, and as women they constantly healed the human race. But that is not their only identity. They are more than that. They are good and bad, they are black and white, they are fat and thin, they are also leaders, professionals, sports women, and above all, they are themselves, and not what the society wants them to be. A society in which women are free is also a liberal society in which men are happier.

Our obsession with sex

'Birds do it, bees do it. Even educated fleas do it. Let's do it...'

Animals are sexual beings and human beings are animals. Human beings have recognized and respected the fact for centuries until some stupid person came up with the idea of chastity – a word that suddenly made sex sound bad. Our taboo about sex is so strong that Cole Porter had to change the lyrics of his song. The original lyrics were – 'Chinks do it, Japs do it, up in Lapland little Laps do it...' That was apparently offensive, even though we all do it! Unfortunately, the worst victims of chastity have been women. Just because they took the pain of giving birth, society rewarded women with the blame of the original sin. Statues of mother goddesses with big breasts and exaggerated sexuality depicting fertility have been discovered all over the world dating back to over 30,000 years. Goddesses like Inanna, Isis, Asherah, Artemis, Shakti, Guanyin and Mazu not only represented fertility, but the power and freedom of women. However, with chastity, all that changed. Female deities were burnt, broken, outlawed and replaced by male gods. As sex was bad, many of these male gods had no option but to take birth by divine magic and not sex. Women and virginity became a holy combination and the only way mother Mary could survive in this new world.

From their childhood, society has brainwashed women to believe that sex is bad, and it became a taboo with time. A 'good' woman was defined as one who had the right to love, but not lust. To lust was to sin. In fact, in medieval Europe, a woman with libido could be labelled as a witch and burnt to ashes. Female libido was considered a disease and doctors like Baker Brown recommended surgical removal of the clitoris to prevent women from such a 'fatal disease'. Men were recommended to have sex with their wives only once in a month, leaving both partners frustrated. While men found solace in prostitutes, women suffered the 'fatal disease'. The only cure for such cases was massage of the pelvic area done by expert physicians. Such treatment often ended with orgasm, thus curing the patient. It was such a serious problem of that time, and a treatment that the physicians did not enjoy doing, that it resulted in the invention of vibrators. In fact, vibrators were just the fifth electrical appliance to arrive at household after the sewing machine, fan, tea kettle and toaster. Necessity was the mother of a machine that replaced husbands.

Despite speaking of sex being a taboo in many societies, it sells like hot cakes. In fact, even hot cakes do not sell close to as much as sex. Sex runs a billion-dollar porn industry. Every second, around 30,000 internet users are glued to pornography. Even though pornography is said to be a product of Victorian England, we find numerous forms of erotic arts in many ancient cultures, including India. Sex is our basic desire that most people cannot suppress for long. Priests and *sadhus*, who claim to have control over their libido, have been often caught for heinous sexual crimes, especially against children. Extramarital affairs have devastated innumerable families around the world. The #metoo revelations are shaking Bollywood up. So, why is sex so attractive? Why do people go to extreme measures to commit an act that has the potential to ruin their lives and that of others?

Sex is the single most enjoyable act on earth. That's how we are programmed to think, especially while in action. One can argue that sex is the reason we are here, and hence evolution programmed us in that way. But we must not forget that sex is not the only method available to life for reproduction. Asexual method of reproduction came first and is still seen in flatworms and many microbes. May be even asexual method of reproduction gave the same pleasure. So whenever the asexual you felt the urge, you could have self-stimulated yourself into two or more parts. That would have been more effective as we could have saved a lot of time (and money) involved in finding (and maintaining) a partner (just for mating). Not only sex drains out our precious nutrient resources, it also means, compared to asexual reproduction, the chances of replication of individual genes are halved, since your kin has only half your genes.

The significance of sex lies in our good old philosopher Charles Darwin's famous quote 'survival of the fittest'. The answer did not come from human beings but from genetically modified yeasts. A study done on yeasts showed that the ones reproducing sexually were hardier, and had better chances of survival under stressful conditions compared to their asexual counterparts. Sexual reproduction gives genetic diversity to the offspring. This simply means that there is plenty to choose from. A sexually reproducing human being can have a choice of an Indian, a Chinese, an African or a white-skinned partner. However, the unfortunate (and virtual) asexually reproducing human being won't have that choice. That choice helps in immune system diversity that keeps us ahead of parasites and pathogens. The variety in the genes caused by sexual reproduction ensures that there would be at least some group of people who will have the right genes to survive a stressful condition. Evolution preferred sexual organisms compared to the asexual ones. The pleasure associated with sex made sure that we are motivated enough to go through the complicated procedure of sex. Even then, not all animals are as sexually adventurous and pervert as humans. So, why did human beings become sex maniacs?

The 'mania' is in our genes. No wonder we share a common ancestry with bonobos and chimpanzees, both of whom are sexually very active. Old taxonomic name of chimps is *P. satyrus*, referring to the myth of apes as lustful satyrs. In terms of sexual activeness, bonobos are one step ahead of chimps. We are not the only 'perverts'. Sex is an essential part of the social relation of this female-centric group of bonobos. Sex is not just between male and female, but with all possible combinations, and their frequency of sex is one of the highest amongst all mammals. Despite the high frequency, the birth rate in bonobos is like chimps. Just like *Homo sapiens*, sex for bonobos is not just a tool for reproduction, but also a means of socializing and having fun. Sex, to them, is an important part of being in a society. It helps them get emotionally attached to the group. We happen to share more than 98% of our genetic profile with bonobos. So it turns out that we had one very hyper sexual common ancestor. There is one possible hypothesis for why this ancestor existed in the first place. Different individuals get different amount of pleasure during sex, which is hereditary. People who got more pleasure had more sex and hence had more children to transfer their genes. On the other hand, people who got less pleasure, had less sex, and hence had fewer children to transfer their genes. Thus, with time, those people who got more pleasure dominated, and the ones who got less pleasure perished. Classic natural selection at play.

Male vs Female libidos

S ex equality does not mean that the urges of both males and females are same. Social psychologist Kristina Durante of the University of Minnesota found in her study that ovulating women buy more revealing clothes. They are, in general, more interested in men than the ones who are not ovulating. In fact, women have been found to be attracted to masculine male faces while ovulating and softer faces during other times of their cycle. This attraction is a natural phenomenon and is governed by the change in biochemistry (hormones and neurotransmitters) inside the brain of ovulating women. Men have stronger sex drive and think about sex more often, says sex expert Tracey Cox, but women can have multiple orgasms and gets more pleasure out of sex while at it. Males are stimulated visually, while women by character. This does not mean that men want sex more than love. While women needs emotional connect for sex, sex is the way to emotional connect for men. This in itself is evolutionary.

Our male ancestors used to know that a woman was grown enough to give birth and is ovulating by visually looking at them. They also needed to know that the woman was healthy. Beautiful and sexy women were both grown up and healthy. That became the male criteria for attraction. This later took an unfortunate turn and resulted in objectification of women. Females, while looking for a strong and healthy male, also needed to ensure that the man would be there for her through the pregnancy and after childbirth. The words and actions of the male had to be loyal and supportive in order to prove that we cared. Unlike males, for females, sex results in pregnancy that lasts for nine months. That is a serious investment of time and energy. Quite naturally, they have higher standards while choosing mates. If the man was a rich strong leader, it was an added bonus. These ancient character traits still continue, even though the necessity of such behaviours might have become irrelevant. Women are still choosier in selecting partners compared to men. Data from dating services show that women were attracted towards one in ten men, while men choose twice that number. Men tend to prefer beautiful women, while women prefer rich men.

Evolution sculpted men's mind and women's body in a way that women attract men once she reaches puberty. Sole purpose of evolution is to ensure that the fittest genes spread. Genes of individuals with the psychology of mating the most spread through natural selection. Human breasts are an example of such a tool that has been carved by evolution. No other animal has such large breasts that stay enlarged right from puberty till death. In other mammals, they enlarge during ovulation or nursing, in order to breastfeed the young. In humans, however, it serves a dual purpose of feeding as well as attracting men. It is a costly price for attraction, considering that breast cancers are the main cause of cancer-related deaths in women. If breasts are removed, the chance of breast cancer in women drops by 95%. Yet, this unnecessary fat has shaped our civilization. Female beauty has created and destroyed many empires. The attraction is so fatal that there are tribes in Cameroon where the breasts of young girls are ironed by their mother so that they are not large enough to gain unnecessary attention. Women's beauty was men's weakness. Men in patriarchal societies did not leave any stone unturned to weaken their biggest weakness. In some places of India, Dalit women were barred from covering their upper body in the past. Tax was collected from these Dalit women if they wanted to cover their bosom. More impertinent was the fact that the amount of tax was proportional to the size of the breast. A Dalit woman from Travancore, named Nangeli, protested against the brutal system in nineteenth century. Instead of paying tax, she cut her breasts and offered it to the tax collector. She died the same day, due to excessive blood loss. Her sacrifice led to the abolishment of breast-tax in Travancore. Her place in now called Mulachiparambu, meaning 'the land of the breasted women'. In Iran, few women opened their hijab to protest against the government. Slut Walk, that started after a police officer in Canada suggested women to avoid dressing like sluts as precaution against sexual assault, spread across the globe. The irony of our society is that in some places women have to revolt in order to cover their bodies, while in other places they have to revolt in order to uncover. Taking a closer look, there is no irony as both protests aren't different. The protests are not about what dress to wear or not to wear, rather it is about having the choice to wear what one likes.

Some authors have described men as just a life supporting system for the penis. In truth, having different urges does not necessarily mean that women have less libido. A study was done by sexologist Dr Chivers on a group of men and women with varying sexual orientation. They were shown erotic video clippings of different types. There were light sensors put in the genitals to measure the blood flow, which indicated excitement. They were also asked to rate their arousal using a keypad. The results were a revelation. Men's measured excitement was predictable and similar to their manual ratings. A straight man was not excited by gay sex and vice versa. Women were more flexible and were excited by most clippings according to the sensor. However, they were more conservative when reporting. Women, by nature, were more fluid in their desires than men. Not surprising, because both men and women are systems that support life. Yet, because of the way society brings up women, they suppress their sexuality. Biology tells them something, while the stories created by society tells them something else. Their body speaks something, and mind speaks something else. When we say that women have a more complex mind than men, how much of that do you think is induced by the contradiction between nature and nurture? Contradictions generate stress, and stress leads to unhappiness.

Are humans monogamous?

Ravi left his friends, family, education and the small town he grew up in, to settle for a small job in the big bustling city of Delhi. This city was not familiar to him and he was nobody here, unlike his hometown where everybody knew him by name. The only solace in his otherwise stressful life was his soul mate Babita with whom he had eloped a month back. Love is a divine feeling. When you are in love, it seems to be the only reality. Everything else becomes secondary. It might seem unfair to reduce such passionate emotions to just biology. Sorry, but that is exactly what I am going to do. Our feelings and emotions are hormone and neurotransmitter driven, organic chemistry, controlled by our brains. It's the testosterone that controls our urge of having sex. It is the chemicals in the brain that gives signal to a person and tells him to be corrupt. It is the chemicals that told Gandhi to be non-violent. It is the same chemicals that make a candle light dinner feel romantic. We can say that we are what hormones and neurotransmitters our brain secretes. Where does love fit in this scheme?

Love is a powerful emotion that has destroyed lives, inspired lives, and evoked finest works of art and literature. There is burst of neurons in our brain the moment we hear the word 'love'. No one can deny the fact that love occupies a dominant space in our brain. How can it not exist? Lust comes from the genes' urge to replicate, while love comes from its want to protect that replication. While lust is entirely biology, love is also about social and cultural bonding that keeps a tribe united. Lust is controlled by the desire part of our brain and love is governed by both desire and emotion. Ancient Greeks identified seven types of love in which only *Eros* comes close to lust. *Eros* is sexual or passionate love. Greeks believed that this kind of 'mad' love ensues when one was struck by Cupid's arrow. The second type of love is named *Philia*, the platonic love of friendship. The love between family members is called *Storge*. *Agape* is the unselfish concern for the welfare of any person or thing, including god and nature. The casual love with no strings attached is called *Ludus*. When love is founded on reason or duty, like arranged marriage, it was called *Pragma*. The last, but not the least, is self-love or *Philantia*. *Philantia* can either be positive acceptance or detrimental self-obsession. One can fulfill different aspects of love from different people. Expecting all kinds of love from one partner can be a stretch. If you wish for it, you may end up like Draupadi, married to at least five different people, if not seven. But, does polygamy come naturally to animals? There are some rodents like the *prairie vole* that appear to be monogamous. Studies done on them showed that their monogamy was entirely controlled by the chemical cupids – oxytocin and vasopressin. When the secretion of these neurotransmitters was reduced, faithfulness was tossed out of the window. For humans, however, it is complicated as our ancestors were not monogamous by nature. However, faithfulness was essential for human survival because of one specific evolutionary change.

Human intelligence and the resulting big head size come at the cost of us giving birth to immature offspring. Before the kids could survive on their own, parents need to protect them, nourish them and teach them survival skills. Unlike other animals, this takes years for human beings. Without the parental bonding, love and faithfulness, human kids would not survive. Love between partners was important for increasing the chance of survival of the offspring, until he or she had grown old enough to defend for himself/herself. Jared Diamond believes that hidden ovulation in human females, and their ability to have sex not just when the woman is ovulating, promotes monogamy. The male can have sex at most times instead of just waiting for his partner to ovulate. This keeps him loyal to one woman, till the kid grows up.

Fisher did some experiments in 1996 to understand the relation between the neurotransmitters and love. Secretion of dopamine is proved to be associated with reward and lust. While dopamine gets you addicted to love, it is norepinephrine that triggers the desperate need to be near one's romantic partner. This bugger makes you stay awake at night and gives you the nervous feeling when you are in love. At the same time, low serotonin level makes one obsessed with one's partner. These are the neurotransmitters that combine to give the 'falling' feeling of first love. Just like rats, longer bonding of love is created by the neurotransmitter oxytocin, produced in the hypothalamus. Vasopressin also seems to have a similar affect. Feeling of love is associated with the reward system in our brain and is mostly outside our control. Interestingly, the same areas in the brain that govern love also govern hate. Love and hate are imprinted in our brains. Does existence of love make marriage a natural choice?

Marriage is a creation of human civilization and it isn't part of natural law. Fornication is how animals breed, and that's how we used to breed. It is stupid to consider it impure. Marriage was probably a product of human insecurity, or a way for strategic alliance. Not surprisingly, the old Anglo-Saxon word for wife meant 'peace-weaver'. None of it sounds divine to me. While marriage itself is not bad, it is a personal choice. In fact, marriage means different things to different tribes/cultures, and not in all cultures, marriage means monogamy. Contrary to Jared Diamond's views, Ryan and Jetha provide some convincing evidence of human beings' promiscuous nature right uptill agricultural revolution, in their controversial book *Sex at Dawn*. Before the agricultural revolution, the tribal societies were small, rarely exceeding 100-200 people. These societies shared responsibilities and all commodities with each other, including sex. These ancient customs still exist among various tribes. There are few modern tribes where young men and women dance together in the evenings as pastime. This helps them choose the most eligible mate, and such pastimes do not necessarily end up in marriage. What is more intriguing is that both men and women in some tribes are allowed to have multiple partners at the same time. Tribes like the Warao of Venezuela and Guyana have customs of sex during particular rituals with whomever they like, even after marriage. The partners were always trusted people in the same tribe. In no way was it casual sex. Just like bonobos, multi-male-multi-female mating in humans was a way of bonding emotionally with each other, creating a strong society. Since there was no way to know who the father of a particular child was, everyone took care of the little ones together. Just because our two closest relatives, bonobos and chimps, and some isolated human tribes that exist today, are promiscuous, it is not enough reason to believe that most of our ancestors were. However, there is one evidence that is difficult to hide, and it lies right between the legs.

The evidence lies in the two ellipsoid male sex glands located inside a pouch of skin. Getting hit in those balls can be painful, and some may even compare the pain to childbirth. They are like your wife, you hurt them once and they would make sure you remember it for a long time. The only reason they hurt so much is because nature wants you to protect them by remembering the pain. Quite rightly so. Those 'family jewels' are extremely important to you. Human testis is ridiculously large in order to hold a large amount of sperm. It is located outside the body to keep the sperms alive at optimal temperature by sagging in summer and contracting in winter. If only one sperm is enough, why do we need such a large amount of sperm? Generation of sperms require a large amount of energy which is an unnecessary waste, unless of course there is sperm competition. Sperm competition happens when the spermatozoa of two or more males race to fertilize an egg. If there is competition between different males to impregnate a particular female, then having large amount of sperm is a matter of survival of one's genes. Species in which sperm competition does not exist, males have tiny testis that is not hanging out shamelessly. Large hanging testis is an evidence of sperm competition, but not the only one. The size of the human penis, with respect to body size, is the highest among all primates. The shape of our penis is such that it can pump out any pre-existing semen during the thrusting motion of intercourse. The thrusting motion relaxes just before ejaculation, giving one's own sperms an advantage in the genetic survival war. In addition to that, the first spurt of semen contains chemicals that not only protect the semen from the chemicals of other men's semen, but is also harmful to its competitors. This characteristic exists only in species where there is sperm competition, or in other words, the female mates with multiple males. Why do you think females take longer to reach orgasm and can have multiple ones? It makes it easier for them to have sex with multiple males at the same time. We see, rather hear, remnants of women's preference for mating with multiple males in 'female copulatory vocalization', a fancy term to describe women moaning during sex. The *Kamasutra* advices, 'As a major part of moaning, she may use, according to her imagination, the cries of the dove, cuckoo, green pigeon, parrot, bee, nightingale, goose, duck and partridge'. Some studies say that the orgasmic sound women makes during intercourse helps excite the man and keeps him loyal, even when they fake it. Meg Ryan did prove a point or two to Harry. However, it would be a very heavy price to pay to just keep one's partner loyal, because the 'oohs' and 'aahs' would attract predators. They won't mind the happy hour buy-one-get-one-free offer for dinner. Vocalization might have helped attract more males, thus aiding in sperm competition. How would that help? Having sperm from different males ensures that the most healthy sperm wins, resulting in healthy offspring. If *Homo sapiens* are naturally polygamous as claimed by Ryan and Jetha, are marriages bound to fail?

Since love was originally meant to ensure that the kid is protected till she or he becomes an adult, it is only natural that the attraction between two individuals reduces with time. This is the leading cause of divorces. We often find lame excuses to justify divorces by blaming each other. We assume that lifelong marriages are normal and divorces are anomaly. When one tries to find a reason why their relationship is not working, they are going to find many. But these reasons are just excuses. The real reason is biology. A marriage based on just love is bound to fail. Love needs to be complimented with trust, respect, acceptance of differences, and commitment. Secretion of love hormones decreases as a relation gets older. The only way to reduce this relationship stress is to understand and accept this biological phenomena, rather than playing a blame game. Once we understand the biology of love, one can work towards a better relationship and play a better game. Staying in love for longer is easy. All one needs to ensure is that the right neurotransmitters continue to be secreted. The good news is that there are proven ways of doing that. One of the best methods is to keep one's sexual life active. Sex elevates testosterone levels and enhances oxytocin and endorphin production, keeping you in love. Other activities proven to secrete dosages of the right neurotransmitters are sharing new experiences, travelling together, romantic strolls and eating out in new restaurants. These small adventures spike the dopamine and adrenalin levels. While none of these are new solutions, we now know why they are important. All you need to do is keep training your brain to fall in love with the same person over and over again, and your heart will oblige. Pamper each other, keep giving pleasant surprises to each other, and more importantly, express how much you love him/her. Once you survive a long term healthy relation, it leads to better health and happiness. Studies have shown that long term partners can better cope with financial set-backs and depressions. It has been confirmed that long term love can erase unhappy memories and even replace them with happy ones. Altered reality makes you unknowingly lie about your past. But then, lying is not a bad thing if it leaves a positive impact on people's lives. Believing in wrong stories, however, can negatively impact our lives.

#MeToo Movement

D an Ariely, in his book *Predictably Irrational*, mentions an
experiment done by asking questions to a group of men
while they were having orgasm. The group was asked the same
set of questions again when they were not in an aroused state. The
conclusion of the experiment was stunning. In an aroused state,
the preference of these men for odd sexual activities, including
having sex with animals, were twice as high. They were 20%
more likely not to have safe sex and five times more likely to slip
a women a drug to increase their chance of having sex when in an
aroused state, than when they were normal. These people, who
are just like you and me, were two entirely different personalities
at two different levels of emotional state. In an aroused state,
there was increased secretion of neurotransmitters that makes
one desperate for sex. Desire takes control while emotion and

intelligence take a back seat. In a normal state, emotions are going to make a person compassionate and less violent, while intelligence will make him/her think about consequences. Similar experiments with women had inconclusive results as women's behaviour is more complex because of cultural influences.

While sexual urge is a natural drive, it is no excuse for sexual crimes. Author of *Against our Will*, Susan Brown miller noted, 'man's discovery that his genitalia could serve as a weapon to generate fear must rank as one of the most important discoveries of prehistoric times, along with the use of fire and the first crude stone axe.' This statement might sound a bit exaggerated and especially unfair to the pre-historic males. Patriarchy was not as common in hunting and gathering societies. But, Susan's sentiments echo the condition of the modern world, and make a valid point. The night of 16th December 2012 shocked the entire nation. Indians suddenly realized that it was not human beings, but humanity that the Mayans predicted that was about to end. A 23-year old girl was brutally gang-raped in a moving bus in the capital of India. She soon succumbed to her injuries. There were protests, both real and virtual, all over the country. Some wanted justice for the girl, some were protesting against the rape crimes and rising violence against women, while others were there because they were afraid of their and their family members' future. The police was definitely tempted by few miscreants, who wanted the police to attack the innocents and make one more case against the government that was already weakened by corruption. The weakness of a non-violent protest is that one small act of violence gives the police enough reason to attack and break down the entire protest. Amongst the pandemonium, one thing was clear, people were concerned, and there were good reasons to be. There has been a staggering eight-fold rise of rape cases in India in the last four decades. A woman is raped every twenty minutes. Delhi topped the chart of rape cases in India with Mumbai a close second. Though the crime is rising, the conviction rate is dropping and stands at just 26%. Rape is a major issue, not just in India, but around the globe. How can we resolve this problem?

There are some myths floating around about rape, and we cannot reduce rape unless we debunk the myths. Human rape is not an aberration. Rape is common amongst other animals too. It is not about males trying to feed their ego or prove that they are stronger. Rape is not a product of patriarchy because rape is equally common in societies and animals which are not patriarchal. Rapists are not people with mental disorder, but normal people who live among us. This makes it so difficult to find the rapists in advance. Rape can sometimes be adapted as a strategy by losers when consenting sex is not available. The skewed sex ratio in India, especially in Delhi, makes this point very important. The lesser the number of females, the more unsafe it becomes for them. It is a bigger issue in a society where there is a strict gender divide. While rape is generally seen as a crime committed by males against females, the number of cases of sexual violence against males is equally significant. Strong patriarchy prevents males from reporting rapes. Most frequent sexual crimes against males, especially children, are committed by males. Sexual crimes by females are also not uncommon. One common myth about male rape victims is that they are never unwilling to have sex, and if they are being raped by a female, then they should feel lucky. Another myth is that a man cannot be raped unless he is willing because he will not have erectile response. Just to make the facts clear, men can also have erections while in stress, and having an erection does not mean male consent to sex. Psychiatric studies have shown that rape and sexual assault can leave men as traumatized as their female counterparts.

While there is a natural desire to procreate, we have the power of emotions and intelligence to keep our desires in check. It is possible if we create the right narrative. Pushing women inside the four walls is not the right story. The more the two genders mingle from the beginning, the more they understand and respect each other. The urge to have sex is natural, the inability to control the urge, or commit an act against someone's consent, is not. Our forced morality that conflicts with our nature confuses us. The key is to teach our children about the importance of consent and respect for every individual. That is what controls the internal urge once we accept that the urge exists. Another factor that can reduce rape cases is enforcement of strict laws. Section 375 of the Indian Penal Code defines rape as penetration, sufficient to constitute the sexual intercourse, necessary to the offence of rape. The term will not be less than 7 years, but it may be for life or for a term which may extend to 10 years. The person shall also be liable to be fined. While the law itself is not strict enough, the implementation is even worse. Even existing law, if enforced properly, will create fear in the mind of offenders. The best solution, however, is the age old method of naming and shaming. This is why #metoo campaign can have a strong influence. Cases of rape and sexual assault are common because it is easy to get away. If we raise the stakes, the incidents will fall.

What makes rape and sexual assaults so brutal is not just the act itself, but also the way society treats the victims. We, as a society, ensure that life becomes hell for the victim and their family. We either avoid them and treat them as outcastes, or shower our sympathies. We keep reminding the victims what they have gone through and make sure that life isn't normal for them again. Who will punish the society that rapes the victim emotionally every day after the act has been committed? In India, more than half of the women believe that it is justifiable for a man to beat his wife. Who will change this mindset? As long as the bride's family will give dowry, as long as the woman becomes the property of the husband's family after marriage, as long as women are not given equal opportunity in the workplace, women will not be independent. As long as women are not independent, they will not get the respect they deserve. The real battle should not be against the government or police, but against the society that promotes gender inequality. It might be a fight against our own family, our own parents or a fight against whom we love. Are we ready for it? As long as we don't fight the evil within us, we will not make our country and the world a safer place for women.

Is sex bad?

I overheard an interesting conversation on my way to Ahmedabad on the Swarna Jayanti Rajdhani. It was a debate between two girls – one was a Jain and the other Muslim. The Muslim girl was surprised, and in fact shocked, when she heard that the Jain girl visits her grandfather, a *Digambara* monk who stays naked all the time. To her, humans did not wear clothes when they lived in the wild. As they became more civilized, they started wearing more and more clothes. Covering the body is a sign of progress, while being naked takes you closer to the wild. She also believed that when a girl is wearing revealing clothes, she is trying to get the attention of men. Evolution wired our brains that way. To her, exposure of flesh triggers the sexual-sensitive part of our brain. She could not understand how an adult girl can see a man naked, that too her grandfather? The Jain girl, on the other hand, could not relate to what the Muslim girl was trying to tell her. To her, advancement of civilization comes through *moksha* or salvation. When you attend that state, you can easily renounce all materialistic pleasure, which includes clothes. Her grandfather has attained that state and hence being naked in front of others does not matter to him. And since she had been seeing her grandfather without clothes from the time she can remember, she feels no difference. They were both tuned to a particular way of thinking, and it was very difficult to change that thought process. Both of them were partly right. The idea of 'beauty' or 'sexy' is the brain's way to attract. That is why you find a person of your own species sexy. If it was a dog or camel instead, there is something terribly wrong with you. By that same logic, a bunny will find a naked and furless Angelina Jolie very ugly. Even though you might want to convince yourself that you dress up just for yourself, your neurotransmitters that are giving you the ideas, have a different plan. You may argue that if beauty is not an absolute entity and only evolution's coding with a purpose, then why does the snow-capped mountain look beautiful? You do not really want to have cute little snow capped babies with it. You are right. Different types of beauty trigger different neurotransmitters. The one triggered by the sight of six pack abs or beautiful girls triggers a different part of the brain than the beauty of the mountains. Maybe you do indeed dress for yourself because it makes you happy. But the concept of beauty is fashioned by our desires. The Muslim girl was right about evolution and how our brain is wired. Your definition of beauty, or being sexy, comes from the biology of attractiveness. It is the same reason why ovulating women buy more revealing clothes.

There is no harm in trying to be attractive. It is a personal choice. With practice like the monks do, that feeling of attraction and lust can be controlled, just like the Jain girl argued. With proper education and training, one can move beyond the taboos of sex.

Human beings have always been uncomfortable getting out of their comfort zone, because out-of-the-zone, their chance of survival gets drastically reduced. Post-agricultural societies created new norms and brought changes in our way of life. New society required new rules and new narratives of morality and justice that were often at odds with millions of years old rules of nature. The new society became uncomfortable with the flexibility of gender; they were uncomfortable with female independence and they were even uncomfortable with sex. Thus, sex became a taboo. While it may have been necessary for the stability of new cultures, the fight against our innate nature and the resulting taboos brought new stresses. There is nothing too serious about sex. It is neither holy, nor a sin. Having sex with multiple partners has been a norm for us during the major period of our existence. It was not a sin because no one was cheating or hurting anybody. Morality is just a social construct. Virginity is neither a quality, nor losing it a sign of coolness. So, let's take it easy. There is no right or wrong way as long as we value consent, respect each other, and are not cheating. It is okay to choose the path that is right for you as long as you are true to yourself. If you want to stay with the one you love for a long time, make sure you work towards it. Complacency murders relationships.

Once we understand each other's nature and respect the differences, we can reduce inequality of all types, including gender 2015 McKinsey Global Institute report estimated that advancing gender equality can add $12 trillion to global GDP by 2025. Equal opportunities would make us more productive and leave behind a positive influence on our society. Mindset is just the way our brain is programmed. If the right stories are reinforced daily, our brain could be rewired and trained to be fair to all. Now that we have some idea of how we came to be, how our faulty sense organs attempt to make sense of everything, and shed some of our prejudices, we are in a position to ask the ancient question, 'Who are we?'

Question 4

Who Are We?

‎❧

'We often know little of who we were, only something of who we are, and nothing of who we may be.'

– Charlie Fletcher, *Silvertongue* (2008)

Being alive

We can unmistakably differentiate between what we think as non-living and the others whom we call as living. The distinction is so clear that even a child can recognize it. Right? Let's think about it once more. Philip Ball, the British science writer, observed that defining life is pointless as there are no boundaries between what is alive and what is not. The boundary is indeed very thin. Indian ancestors thought that everything is made of air, water, wood and fire, in different proportions; and according to modern science, everything is made of sub-atomic particles called protons, electrons and neutrons, or strings with different vibration patterns. Since the basic ingredient of everything is the same, how come living things got separated from the non-living? At the time of the Big Bang, was everything non-living and life just happened as a chance event later? Or, was life itself created with the Big Bang? Is there indeed such a distinct difference between living and non-living, or is the line thinner than we would care to acknowledge? Plants were considered as non-living things until 1899 when Sir Jagadis Chandra Bose noted convincing evidence of life. Life has been found in extreme places like in the mid oceanic ridges where no one expected living things to survive. Life here exists without sunlight, supported by vented hydrothermal fluids driven by heat from magma chambers! Then look at the viruses, are they living or non-living? They evolve and reproduce, but not without the help of host cells. Where do we draw the line?

There are six essential criteria to be classified as a living thing: intake of nutrients, metabolism, excretion of waste products, reproduction, death, and response to stimuli. What one considers as nutrient varies depending on who is taking in the nutrient. Sunlight, for example, is a nutrient for a plant, but to us it is something that helps us tan our skin. There are micro organisms that survive on faeces, which can be poison to others. There are bacteria in the lower crust that eat rocks, something that would kill us. Once we intake the nutrients, we convert it by complex chemical reactions to something more useful for our body. This process is called metabolism. It creates other products that are useless for us and hence we simply throw them out. The same thing is done by our planet earth; it eats sunlight and excretes excess heat. Consider the stars. They suck in hydrogen gas into their stomach (core), perform some chemical reactions, and then excrete the heavier atoms in form of stellar winds or violent stellar explosions. Taking in nutrients, performing metabolism and excreting waste products is just physics and chemistry and are not unique to living things. Now let us look at the cycle of birth and death. If the ability to give birth was necessary criteria to be a living being, what would you call a mule? Reproduction does not mean sex; it is just creation of new ones. All some creatures have to do to reproduce is divide themselves into two, like amoebae. Some plants can grow new plants from their broken stems, not unlike crystals. Genes might be unique to living forms in our world, but it might not be a necessary criterion to consider an alien form as living. New stars can form from older stars. Why would that not be called as reproduction? Sometimes planets can explode and reform into many smaller planets. Every star (or even planet) has a life cycle from birth to death, just like the things we consider living, the only difference is the time frame. So, the circle of birth and death is not a distinguishing criterion either. The only possible distinction we are left with, that separates living things from non-living, is our sense of perception and the fact that we respond to stimuli. One may argue that living things behave in self-preserving ways to further their life by responding to stimuli. A plant grows towards light and sprouts its roots towards water. A non-living rock would not care to move even when you crush it. But then, the sense of perception is different in different things. Some animals sense the world in ways that we cannot imagine, for example through pheromones, magnetic fields and echolocations. We can never be sure if our galaxy perceives in its own way or not, just like a bacteria inside your body is not sure of the fact that you perceive or not when it crushes your cells. Things respond to stimuli only if there is a need to respond. The earth has no need to respond when you walk over it, just like the plants or trees which do not slap you when you sit on their branches. Now think of the double-slit experiment. The electrons did respond to the presence of the observer. Can it be considered as living? What if the entire universe was alive in all possible scales?

Life and environment are intricately related and Gaian Hypothesis propose that both of them co-evolve together. Life influences the environment and the environment influences the biota. Together it forms one complete system, just like us and the three kilos of bacteria in our body form a complete interdependent system. This idea was originally proposed by James Lovelock as the earth feedback hypothesis. Lovelock received his fair share of criticism, and his hypothesis has long been ignored. Recently, however, Gaian Hypothesis is regaining its popularity. There is enough evidence to suggest that the global temperature, ocean salinity, and other life supporting conditions on earth self-regulate itself influenced by the action of living things. This whole system is called the 'Gaian System' that blurs the difference between the living and the non-living. One can even go to the extent of saying that life is just a surface process happening on earth that does not distinguish between castes, religions or race.

Adi Sankaracharya, a higher-caste Brahmin and a great Indian philosopher of the 8th century, was once in the holy city of Varanasi. As he was walking towards the River Ganges, he found his path being blocked by an untouchable. The untouchable, a person belonging to the lowest strata of Indian society, had four white dogs with him. The touch of an untouchable was considered impure and Sankara, fearing that he might touch him, ordered the untouchable to move away. Undeterred, the untouchable replied, 'Why should I go away, and from what? Is it the physical body, or the spirit that you want to move? If it is the body, then all bodies are made of the same stuff, why should one body get away from the other? If it is the spirit, then the spirit is non-dual. It is here and everywhere, from what then it should go away? Is there a difference between the sunlight reflected from the holy Ganges and from the pools in the streets where the untouchables live?'

The great priest had no answer. The holy was humbled by the lowly. That incident changed Sankaracharya's view about life. The great sage then went around India teaching the concept of *Advaita Vedanta*. 'Self' is same as the ultimate reality, and the distinction between living and non-living is hazy. That begs the question, who are 'we'?

'Who are we?' is one of the most primitive questions we have been asking ourselves – a proof of us being conscious beings. Philosophers and scientists have been asking this question for thousands of years, but the perfect answer has eluded us. I do not think there is a perfect answer. In fact, I don't think that there is a single answer. This question can be tackled from various angles, because we are many things. We are a form, a code and even an information. Who we are, depends on which story we prefer.

A form

Some of us associate our self with our body. Our body is made of numerous small cells. Your cells are dying as I speak, and are being replaced by new ones. In an average adult human, about 50-70 billion cells die daily by natural process of apoptosis, or programmed cell death. When the cell is stressed enough, or receives the signal of death from the nearby cells, it commits suicide. The whole process is like a 'Game of Thrones' episode. The cell activates initiator caspases, which activate executioner caspases, which then kill the cell by cutting the DNA, RNA, proteins and carbohydrates of the cell into bits and pieces. In short, your cells are thrashed and the pieces are served to the nearby phagocytic cells by the process called efferocytosis. As a result, all traces of your cells are gone, as if it was never there. The body you were born with is long dead. As an adult, the cells that make you now are over fortieth descendent of the egg cell that you started with. We replace about 98% of our atoms every year. This process of cell division, useful for growth and replacement of injured cells, is called mitosis. If you are your body, then you have already died many times. We do not shed tears for our cells because it keeps us healthy. Death is nature's way of keeping itself healthy. Chemical reactions are constantly happening in our cells. They are powered by glucose (from the foods we eat) and oxygen (from breathing) that forms energy carrying molecule ATP. This energy is used for growth, repair and reproduction. These energy molecules must move from an ordered state to disordered state by diffusing towards low concentration or breaking down randomly as per the second law of thermodynamics. The cell's job is to prevent that from happening and keep things in order to make sure that the biological processes does not stop. Death happens when we lose the battle against entropy. The trick to eternity is to find ways to keep entropy in check.

Cells, like everything else, are made of atoms. Lord Kelvin once demonstrated how small atoms are. Let's say you are in the Kerala coast and you could mark water molecules in a glass full of water; and then pour the water in to the vast ocean and stir it to mix the molecules evenly. Then you fly to the Kohala coast on the other part of the world and take out a glass of water from the ocean, you will still have about hundred marked molecules in your glass. This is how small atoms are, and nature recycles the molecules vigorously over time. Our cells are being disassembled and recycled all the time. The new ones that are growing and replacing the old ones are being made from the atoms of something or someone else. It is a continuous cyclic process that we are not consciously aware of. When you are at home, I want you to find the biggest mirror. Stand in front of it and look at yourself very carefully. You are looking at yourself, yourself that is made up of cells, and cells that are made up of atoms. Look at yourself and remember this. The atoms that make you were once part of a distant star. They were once part of the mighty dinosaurs. A part of you definitely belonged to Buddha, Genghis Khan, and even Shakespeare. You are a reincarnation of all these great legends and more. Every inch of you is immortal if you think that you are what you are made of. What gives these unconscious atoms the urge to replicate and survive?

A code

From atoms form DNAs, and from DNAs form genes. DNAs are the replicators that defines life. Scientists like Richard Dawkins believe that the true us is our selfish genes. Our body is just its means of survival. Different genes ally together and create our body as a 'survival machine' to fight against the competitor genes. For example, the homeotic genes regulate development of our body parts. Any error in this particular genetic code might mean having a wrong body part in the wrong place. Different codes results in different looks, which becomes our identity. Be it your fingerprints, or your retina scan, your uniqueness lies in your genes. Our genes decide whether I will be an unholy human or a holy cow. It is the same code that decides if I can get dowry after marriage or get killed before birth. The sole purpose of the codes is to survive. We receive it from our parents and transfer them to our kids.

We started in an orgasmic bliss. After which the winner sperm, carrying half of the father's genetic material, ran and fused with the egg, carrying half of the mother's genetic material. Apart from the 23 chromosomes from the father, we get everything else from our mother. Not just the proteins, ribosomes, nutrients and membranes, but also the mitochondria come from the egg. Siddhartha Mukherjee aptly wrote that the sperm is no more than a glorified delivery vehicle for male DNA – a genome equipped with a hyperactive tail. Our body dies a million deaths, but we as codes evolve and continue our battle of survival. In fact, the total human gene pool is not that diverse. It is amazing how most people are related though genes. Adam Rutherford, using some basic mathematics, claim that we are all decedents of royalty. A white European will be related to Charlemagne, and Asian to Genghis Khan, and an African to Nefertiti! Which royal blood do you have? The group of genes that had created human beings has suffered countless mutations and survived innumerable natural selections to become us. They became faster and smarter, evolved from being helpless prey to becoming the deadliest predator.

Genes determine our personality more than the environment we grow up in. It is the book of our life. If organisms are cities, the cells are the buildings. The nucleus inside the cell is the library room. The nucleolus is the bookshelf and the chromosomes are the books. Human beings have 46 such books in the bookshelf. The DNAs that make the chromosomes are the pages of the book. Each page has information about the organism it has created, and it is written in its own language. The genes, which are a pair of nucleotites, are the sentences written in the language of ATCG. The genes not just make us from the dust, but also control all our behaviour. Anxious behaviour, depression, trauma, alcoholism, and high-risk behaviours have all been linked to one such sentence written in the ATCG language. The sentence is a single gene called 5HTTLRP. Research was done on more than 800 sets of identical and non-identical twins in Edinburgh University to understand the role of genetics in shaping a person's character. The study showed that identical twins were twice as likely to share same personality traits as compared to non-identical twins, even though they grew up in similar environments. Recent studies have also shown that genetics play a key role in determining 'the big five' personality traits – openness to experience, conscientiousness, extra version, agreeableness and neuroticism (OCEAN). It is still not understood which genes control which type of personality. In most likelihood, a combination of multiple genes affect each personality trait.

Genes also have memories. It can imprint or erase chemical marks on itself to memorize any drastic change in the environment that threatens its existence. That would explain why some new-born animals know things that they never learned, like camouflage from enemies. Our survival instincts may have come from the memories in the genes. Recent studies have brought forth epigenetic markers that changed genetic expression because of some kind of environmental stress. Epigenetic markers are set of alterations in the DNA without changing its sequence. It tells the gene how it will express itself. Epigenetic markers are like the styles of a sentence. They could be underlined, italicized, made bold or highlighted to store different cellular memories.

Even though the genes in all the cells in your body are the same, it is the epigenetic markers that tell them which cells will be the liver cells, which one will grow as the brain cell, or kidney cells, or muscles, etc. In a well-studied case from Western Netherlands, where the Nazis cut off food supply in the winter of 1944, it was established that the kin of those who survived the Dutch famine became diabetic prone. During the famine, also called 'Honger winter' (hunger winter), the body adjusted to better use of the little nutrients available. Stress in the environment caused an epigenetic imprint in the gene. The gene was then transferred to the children. Even when the children were not suffering the famine, the body still remembered the drought and increased the sugar in the body. I wonder if the terrible diabetes problem India suffers is related to the policies of British Raj that led to innumerable famines. Epigenetic changes can at times be fatal, and result in terminal illness like cancer. However, it is not a single gene mutation, but cumulative effects of ten to hundreds of genes that produce a medical condition.

Errors in the genetic code can not only cause disease, but also determine the age at which the disease will occur. Some evolutionary biologists think that death itself is written in our genes. There is more to ageing and death than the 'free radicals', the normal by-product of ageing, which cause cellular damage. Any mutation that creates genes that results in death at an early age, before one is able to reproduce and pass on the gene, will soon be eliminated from the system. The genes that cause disease, ageing and death at an older age, after the gene has been transferred to the next generation, tend to accumulate over the years of evolution. These genes that trigger old age and cause death, are present within all of us. That is the reason why we die. Our fate is written in these codes. If you are the code that makes you, then you were present at the beginning of life and will be there till life goes extinct. But, are genes conscious? How do they create our sense of identity?

An information

Some say, 'You are what you think'. The truth is, 'You are what you remember'. Suppose I knew magic and was able to erase all your memories.

Abracadabra…

Woooshh…

Your mind is a blank slate now. Your religion means nothing to you. Your country means nothing to you. Even you family means nothing to you. The 'form' you is here and the 'code' you is here. But the 'information' you is dead as your memories about yourself are erased. And along with it, the concept of you in your mind. Others can still relate to you through their memory. Once their memory of you is selectively erased, the information about you will be completely lost, and you will be completely forgotten. Your identity is encoded in the information about you. It is that information that gives us the sense of identity.

Memories are just electro-chemical informations stored in the brain. Scientists like Ramirez and Liu have been able to not just copy these informations, but even transfer memories of one rat to another. Recently, researchers from UCLA were successfully able to transfer memory of shock between marine snails by injecting RNA, the cellular messenger, with the necessary information. This works because memories are not only stored in the synapses as thought earlier, they are also stored in the nucleus of the neurons. This stored information can be copied and also transferred back into the neurons. A current study by Marc Schieber and Kevin Mazurek, with the University of Rochester Medical Centre, Department of Neurology and the Del Monte Institute for Neuroscience, showed the possibility of injecting information directly into the brain of monkeys. This has big implications. In the future, it could be possible to store human memory in memory banks by replicating the information from our brain. This prediction might be a bit of a stretch, considering that human brains are much more complex than snails or rats. But the challenge we have today is not in the theory, but only the practical implementation. It will eventually happen, it is just a matter of time.

Let us do a thought experiment based on the valid theory. If I store my memory in a memory bank when I am 40 years old. I die when I am 70 years. A couple of decades later, my memory is restored into a person who has lost all his memories. So this guy wakes up... hold on... actually I wake up in a new body, still 40 years old, half a century later. Think about it for a bit. Let the idea sink. The 'code' me is transferred to my kids, the 'form' me is recycled and is now part of something else (rather

many things) but the 'information' me is still alive. It would be like a body possessed by my ghost. One can now think of oneself as separate from the body. That memory might as well be defined as consciousness or the soul. It would be beyond genetics or biology, as memories are incorporeal and separate from the body. Like the definition of soul, memories makes you who you are and can live long after the body is dead. Unlike soul, however, memories are scientifically proven. Memories are just electrochemical patterns. The *Bhagavad Gita* is right when it says, 'nothing dies' because a pattern is not even a thing.

It would be interesting to see how the genetic identity of the body conflicts with the mental identity of the memories. As of now, there is no way of knowing that. Memories are controlled by our desires, emotions, and intelligence, which in turn is guided by our genetics. Memories must depend on the genes. By copying memories shaped by a particular set of genes to another body made by different set of genes may result in conflict and depression. But that is a problem for another era. Interestingly, identifying oneself as memory would mean that there is no particular self, because the same memory can be copied into multiple bodies. That will create multiple identities of one person having a shared past, but a different future. Also, as was done with the poor rats, part of memory of one person can be transferred to another person with existing memories, thus creating a chimera of information. The concept of unique identity now gets obscured.

Multiple personality disorders (MPD) are something similar and very common. It is also information about more than one personality in the same body. MPD highlights the

separation between mind and body. Have you ever lost your temper and behaved very rudely with someone? Later, you may have felt that it was not you. Evolution fashioned a complex human brain that has multiple components. Sometimes they live in complete harmony, and at other times those components comes in conflict with each other. Such conflicts create identity crises. *Three Faces of Eve* is a Joanne Woodward starring film released in 1957. It was a first of its kind movie based on the true story of a person named Chris Costner Sizemore. She suffered from MPD. MPD has been a topic of debate in the scientific community for ages. While it was widely accepted in America, MPD got its share of resistance from Britain. With time, however, MPD became widely accepted as more and more case like that of Chris made headlines. Chris had more than twenty personalities and this destroyed her married life. Her MPD was a reaction to severe childhood trauma. Other common causes of MPD are prolonged physical, emotional, or sexual abuse. Chris was finally cured by a Virginia doctor named Tony Tsitos. Thankfully, the rest of her life was pretty uneventful until she died of heart attack when she was 89. Since Chris, many cases of MPD came to the forefront, along with the report of one particular case claiming 4,000 alter-egos. Each ego has a separate memory about itself, and thus separate personalities living in the same body. At any particular moment, you are that part of the memory that is active at that moment.

Neuroscience experiments have proven that the right and the left brain have different characters. Corpus callosum is the connection between the two brains, and in some patients, this has to be removed through surgery, thus severing the connection.

When one such patient was asked about career choice, his left hemisphere answered draftsman while the right hemisphere wanted to be an automobile racer. It was also concluded from surveys of these patients that the left hemisphere was mostly atheist, while the right claimed to be a believer. This shows the complexity of our mind, and thus diversity of our character.

I believe we all have at least two different personalities, one being instinctive and the other being acquired. Instinctive personality (IP) is the genetic traits that we were born with. Our basic instincts that arise out of our desires are part of IP. Desires and motivations can also be acquired over the years as information in our memories, but the dominant control over it is IP. Our acquired personality (AP) develops as we grow. AP is not just what we perceive ourselves as, but also what we want others to perceive us as. AP dominates our emotional behaviour and our acquired knowledge or intelligence. Those who have suffered mental/physical abuse as a child might develop multiple APs. Comparing it to Sigmund Freud's structural model of the psyche, IP is comparable to Id and AP to superego. Freud reasoned that we live our life trying to balance between Id and superego with help of our ego. Superego, or AP, is where the mnemes are copied and spread.

Daniel Kahneman's book *Thinking Fast and Slow* introduces us to the two systems in the mind: System-1 and System-2. He defines them as below:

'System-1 operates automatically and quickly, with little or no effort and no sense of voluntary control.

'System-2 allocates attention to the effortful mental activities that demand it, including complex computations. The operations of System-2 are often associated with the subjective experience of agency, choice, and concentration.'

Kahneman demonstrates the presence of the two systems with help of a simple maths problem. The total price of a bat and a ball is 1$ 10 cents. If the bat costs 1$ more than the ball, what is the price of the ball? The instinctive answer that most people give is 10 cents. System-1 is answering for you, if that's your answer. After doing careful calculations, one finds out that the actual price of the ball is half of it. Those who curbed their instinct (System-1) to think about the correct answer were governed by System-2. System-1 is controlled dominantly by IP, while System-2 is controlled dominantly by AP.

Most of the stresses in our life arise from the conflict between AP and IP, between our heart and mind if you want to put it that way. It is important for us to understand these two personalities that exist within us so that we can make a healthy balance between the two. The act of murder or rape is most likely to be controlled by IP than AP. 'Thinking from your heart' is not always the morally correct decision. However, it is IP that decides whether to fight or take flight, it is IP that makes you fall in love without reason and it is IP that tells you to be in the present and enjoy your life. IP is neither your guardian angel nor a devil. It is the way you want it to be. AP is the stories one learns over the years. It is influenced by our family, school, and the environment that we grow up in. It teaches us not to cheat, not to hurt others, and not to look at thy neighbour's wife. AP can be either governed by social norms or market norms. The warm and fuzzy social norms give us a sense of community, and is important between friends and family. Market norms govern the decisions we take professionally, and generally involves money or something of value to barter. As long as we do not mix the two, like expecting monetary gains in return of love or love in return of professional success, we will do well. These lessons are essential for us to be part of our society.

Depending on our social conditions we create a mental image of 'ourselves'. We tend to believe that there is an absolute unique us. We develop this concept of 'ourselves' right at infancy and it can influence the choices we make in our life right till the very end. AP gives us an identity and it is not a bad thing as long as we understand that it is nothing but an 'essential' myth. Others also have impressions about us, and each person will paint you in a different character. None of those characters will match the character that you have in mind about yourself. The moment we become too rigid about our identity, we lose our minds like the religious fanatics. Religion, nationalism, casteism, etc, are all part of our AP that shapes our identity. Thinking too much about these identities might not be a good idea because most of the time when you over-think, you start to create fictitious situations and unnecessarily worry about your unknown future. Sometimes it is better to just be, let IP take over (as long as you do not harm anyone).

When we realize that we have different personas and understand the strength and weakness of each, we can learn to control them. We can use them the way we want and reduce the conflicts. It is important to mention here that the different personalities are not entirely split. They are interconnected and influence each other. Peace is when both AP and IP dance in the same rhythm. We often build an image in our minds about who we are, about our character. Now we can probably appreciate the complexity of our character(s) and the fact that there is more than one 'us'. There is more to 'us' than our perception about ourselves. The more you try to discover yourself, the more you are going to be surprised. Let us now take the next step towards that discovery.

Many roads

Ramkrishna Paramhansha Dev, the great sage from Bengal, once said that, *'Joto mot totopoth'*. It literally translates to, 'there are as many paths to god (or success) as there are opinions'. When I first read that as a kid, I discarded it as a whimsical fantasy. How can one find god (or achieve success) by just sitting at home and eating pizza, if that is what one wishes? There must be a mistake in that statement. As my hair turned grey, I realized that the mistake was not with the statement, but with my understanding of it. He did not mean that you get what you want by travelling any random path. What he meant was that there are multiple ways to get to where you really want. Both the path and the destination are in the mind. Each one of us have a unique and different mind set, and thus both the path and the destination in each of our mind is different. If you choose the path that suits you and walk the distance, you will reach your goal.

We want a lot of things in our life like money, success, happy family, big car, comfortable house, good job, self-actualization, salvation, etc. But what we need is happiness. All our 'wants' mean nothing if they do not make us happy. Money cannot make you happy, but it can buy you things that can make you happy; and if it does not, then what is money worth? If you have a good job but a bad boss who makes your life miserable, what's the point of having that job? You won't be charitable if it is not making you happy. It is same with everything else. At the end of the day, we need to be happy. If we fix our goal at happiness, then what are the ways we can be happy? You will find many motivational books from experts telling you different magical formulae to achieve happiness. Some would say 'follow your heart', others would tell you to 'believe in yourself'; 'information and planning' would be the mantra for some, while still others would suggest the age-old formula of 'hard work'. Detaching oneself for all materialistic pleasures could also be a path. Which one works? Rather, the more pertinent question would be, which one works for you? That one powerful sentence by Ramakrishna answers the question more eloquently than all the self-help books put together. There is no one path to happiness. Each one of us has our own private road to it. The question is how do we find our road?

If we want to answer that question, we first need to understand our mind. Understanding the complex mind is not an easy task. Attempts have been made by scientists, philosophers and even the religious leaders to make sense of our complex mind for centuries. Christian Wolfe in 1730s classified human mind into the *facult as cognoscitova* – knowledge and belief, and the *facultasappetiva* – desire. Couple of decades later, Moses Mendelssohn added a third dimension – affect – that had to do with feelings and emotions. These three dimensions of the human mind were reinforced by Kant in the late 18th century. He proposed, 'three absolutely irreducible faculties of the mind' are knowledge (or cognition), feeling (or emotion), and desire (or motivation). While classifying our complex minds into pigeon holes is difficult, and most likely imperfect, classification makes it much easier for our symbol-centric brain to understand. All attempts at classifying our mind generally fits the three end-members of desire-emotion-cognition pretty well.

Neuroscientist Paul D. MacLean's Triune Brain Theory classifies brain into three parts. The most primitive part is called the reptilian brain. It controls the vital functions that help us survive, including the heart rate, breathing, body temperature and balance. In other words, it controls our desires. The main structures of reptilian brain are brain stem and cerebrum. The next part of the brain that evolved is the palaeo-mammalian brain. It is responsible for emotions and its main structures are hippocampus, amygdala, and the hypothalamus. Neo-mammalian brain (or primate brain), i.e. the neocortex, is the latest to evolve. Our cognitive abilities and intelligence are derived from this part of the brain. Cognition is a process of acquiring information or knowledge through senses and understanding the universe with the help of that information, thought and experiences. Emotions and desires are related, but not the same. Emotions are strong feelings derived from one's circumstances, mood or relationship with others. It depends a lot on cultures and the way one grows up. Desires, on the other hand, are mostly derived from basic physical needs. One can be ruthless and unemotional in order to fulfil his or her desires. Our every thought is guided by these three dimensions of our mind. The strength of each dimension is different in different persons, and it can even vary with time in a single person. That is the reason why we can have more than one character. The final decision that a person takes depends on where in the Cognition-Emotion-Desire (C-E-D) triangle (Figure 1) the person's mental state is at that moment.

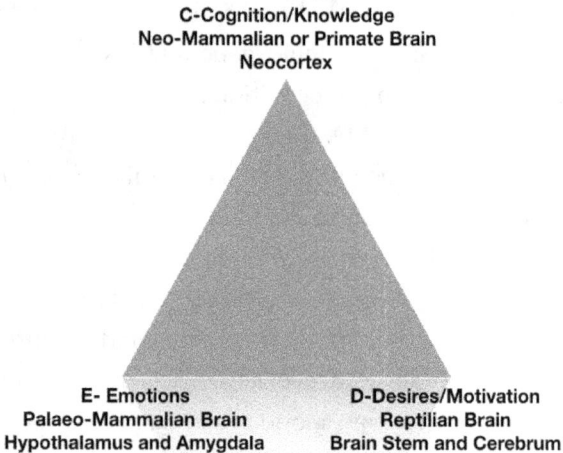

C-Cognition/Knowledge
Neo-Mammalian or Primate Brain
Neocortex

E- Emotions   **D-Desires/Motivation**
Palaeo-Mammalian Brain   **Reptilian Brain**
Hypothalamus and Amygdala   **Brain Stem and Cerebrum**

Figure 1 C-E-D Triangle of Human Mind

Daniel Kahneman'sSystem-1 dominates the D Vertex of the triangle while System-2 dominates the opposite E-C edge (Figure 2). Similarly, the C Vertex is dominated by logic, planning and objective considerations while the E-D edge is dominated by the emotions of feeling, compassion, and perception of the world on the go. Those who are introverts lie on the E Vertex, while the opposite C-D edge is dominated by the extroverts. Where do you think you lie in that triangle?

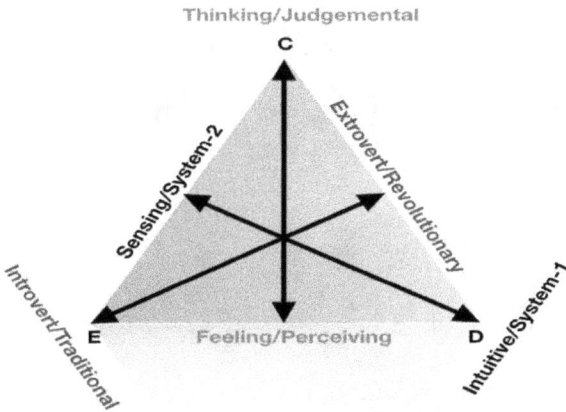

Figure 2: Different Personalities

Hacking your brain

Neuroscientist Antonio Damasio's ground-breaking experiment has shown that human beings are unable to take decisions without emotions. There are times when instinctive decisions help and your gut feelings come true. However, if one's decision is driven by too many emotions, or even personal desires, then the decision taken will mostly be a wrong one. At times, such rash decisions can ruin one's career. To take the correct decision, one has to be in a mental state where the three dimensions of the mind are in harmony. One has to be detached enough to remove any personal bias from affecting the decision, and at the same time, one has to be involved enough to take the decision. Since there is no term to define such a state, I will take the liberty to call it 'intached' state – involved in a detached way. Once we reach the *intached* state, can we hack our brain?

Studies have shown that the brain has the ability to create new neural pathways and enhance our cognitive abilities, making us the way we want to be. This is what gives us the ability to hack our brain. Professor Schaefer has established that forced laughter can turn one into a happy person. As stated by him, 'Once the brain signals the body to laugh, the body doesn't care why. It's going to release endorphins; it's going to relieve stress as a natural physiological response to the physical act of laughing.' There are many proven methods of hacking your brain to get positive benefits. One of the oldest and best methods is yoga and meditation. In the regular state, our brain controls us. Self-actualization can be achieved by hacking the brain to make it do what you want.

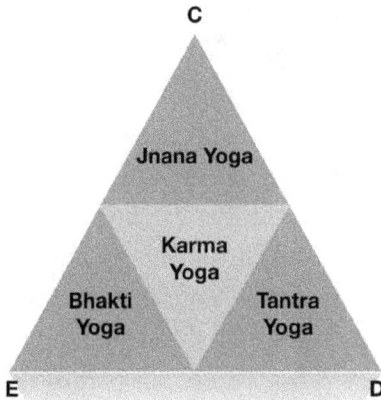

Figure 3: Different Paths of Ancient Indian Philosophy

The analysis of human characters and its variety was understood and appreciated by our ancestors. They realized that there are many ways of achieving self-actualization, depending on one's character. Interestingly, the ancient philosophies that were born out of observation of human behaviours still works if we modify them a bit and make them relevant to our modern context. This paragraph is an attempt towards that. For the people who are emotional, people of heart, there is *Bhakti Yoga* (Figure 3). With complete devotion to something one believes in, he/she can achieve success. The strength they need to utilize is the power of belief and their feelings for others. These groups of people can be moody, and can get easily stressed. They also prefer affiliations, and that could make them conservative, religious, nationalistic or holding on to any specific ideology that helps them get affiliated to a particular group. Such individuals could be tilted towards right wing of political spectrum. Emotion dominated people are good family men and can be very caring. For people of intellect, the path proposed was *Jnana Yoga*. It is about achieving success through sheer knowledge and thinking. Their success is achieved by cutting preconceived notions with sharp logic. These personalities can be judgmental about others and blunt to the point of hurting others' sentiments. They could be geeks, generally liberal, and fall in between left and right wing political ideologies. For those guided by desires, there is the path of *Tantra Yoga*. This is not part of the original *yogas*, but I believe it fits well in here. The success of those falling in this part of the triangle comes by following their instincts. They have a strong sense of purpose and a need to achieve fame. Such people can go crazy and take extreme steps if their desires are not fulfilled. While they may prefer power and fame, these people are also revolutionaries who challenge orthodoxy. Politically, they would be left oriented. For those who lie in the middle of the triangle, the proposed path is that of *Karma Yoga*. They can achieve success by following their duties sincerely and honestly. Meticulous planning and hard work are their key strengths. They can balance well between personal and professional life, but might be too routine and reluctant towards any drastic change.

The term 'self-actualization' was first used by Kurt Goldstein in 1939 as 'the tendency to actualize, as much as possible, [the organism's] individual capacities' in the world. In such a state, an organism has realized its full potential. Achieving self-actualization, says Goldstein, was the ultimate aim of any organism. The reason we want to achieve it is because it is the state in which one finds happiness, bliss and/or success. Abraham Maslow believed that self-actualization is at the top of the hierarchy of needs of human beings. He wrote in *Motivation and Personality* (1954), 'A musician must make music, an artist must paint, a poet must write, if he is to be ultimately at peace with himself. What a man can be, he must be. This need we may call self-actualization.' However, in order to achieve it the basic needs have to be fulfilled.

Maslow defined four basic needs as shown in Figure 4, also called the deficiency needs or d-needs. D-needs consist of physiological needs, safety needs, love and belonging needs and the need for self-esteem. The most basic is the physiological needs, without which we would not survive. It includes food to eat, water to drink, air to breath, sex to continue our progeny, clothing and shelter, and sleep. Once physiological needs are relatively satisfied, the next dominant need is the need for good health, security, employment and money, collectively called the safety need. We may be able survive without safety, but with a lot of stress and trauma. Such frustrations can drag us down to a situation where we would not be able to fulfill our physiological needs as well. Once safety needs are relatively satisfied then the social belonging need dominates. It comes from friends, family and intimate relations. Human beings are social animals. Social belonging gives us the feeling of love and being part of a group. When this need is not fulfilled, one feels lonely and depressed. The last level of d-need is that of self-esteem. Maslow described two levels of esteem, higher and lower. The need of respect from others falls in the lower version. This includes need for status, power, achievement, recognition, fame, etc. The higher version manifests itself as the need for self-respect. Esteem gives one the feeling of accomplishment and boosts self-confidence. Without it, one develops inferiority complex. Once these basic needs are fulfilled, then one is prepared to achieve self-actualization.

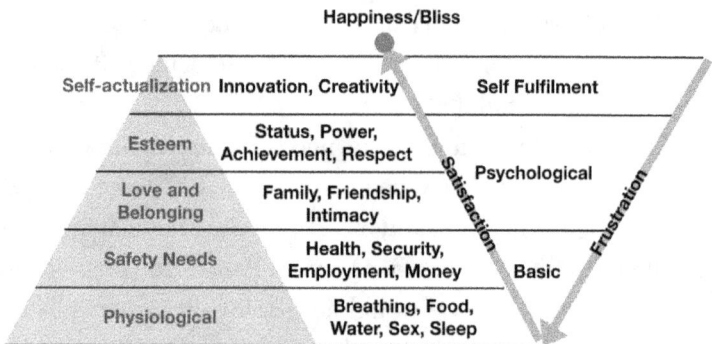

Figure 4 Maslow's d-needs

Maslow's pyramid of human needs is not a lot different from that mentioned in the ancient Indian texts. Accordingly, the four goals of life or *Purusartha* are *kama* (sex), *artha* (wealth), *dharma* (duties) and *moksha* (salvation). In the broad sense, *kama* signifies desire, wish, passion, emotions, pleasure of the senses, the aesthetic enjoyment of life, affection, or love, with or without sexual connotations. It equates to the physiological needs of Maslow. *Artha* includes wealth, career, employment, financial security and economic prosperity. This compares to the safety needs. *Dharma* signifies the right way of living. It includes both the psychological needs. The final stage of *moksha* is the equivalent of self-actualization.

By merging the C-E-D triangle of human mind with Maslow's triangle of needs, we get the Triangular Pyramid of Mind (TPM) (Figure 5). The TPM is a guide to achieving bliss or happiness or success or self-actualization, whichever way one wants to define it. The ancient Indian texts describe five sheaths that one needs to control to achieve self-actualization. They are quite similar to Maslow's d-needs. The outer most of the sheaths is called *virat* or the gross body. These are the basic physiological needs required for survival. One who is controlled by his/her gross body is in the state of *annamaya* and is concerned mainly about food and other outer pleasures. As mentioned in *Patanjali* yoga sutras, this gross body can be brought under control by *yamas* (morality), *niyamas* (personal observances) and *yoga asana* (body postures or exercise). *Yamas* teaches compassion for all living things, commitment to truthfulness, commitment to not stealing, controlling one's sensual activities, including sex and neutralizing the desire to acquire and hoard wealth more than one requires. *Niyamas* are more personal than *yamas* and literally translates to rules or laws. This includes practice of cleanliness, modesty and content, disciplined use of energy by being attentive to all that we do, self-study, and setting aside some time for achieving self-actualization. One can think of it as taking control of the daily chores of life by eating well, breathing well, sleeping well and exercise. This will fulfil the basic physiological needs and help one control his/her desires.

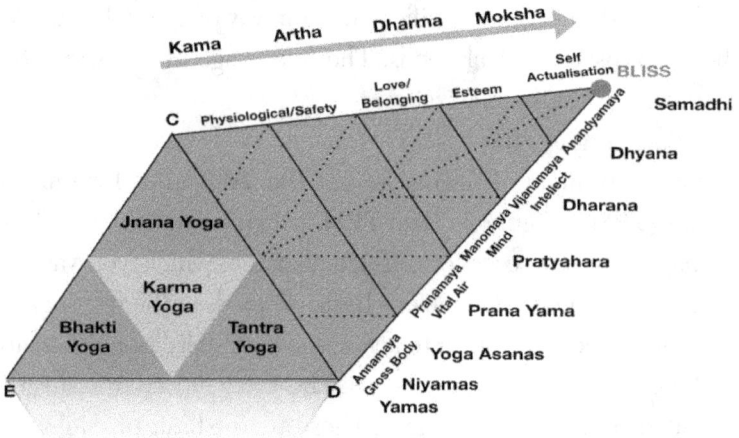

Figure 5: Triangular Pyramid of Mind

Once gross body is under control, one can go to the next stage of controlling the more subtle body called *hiranyagarbha*. *Hiranyagarbha* is subdivided into the vital air, mental and intellectual, in the order from gross to subtle. One who is controlled by the vital air is said to be in the stage of *pranamaya*, where he/she tries to stay alive by protecting and defending. It is through *pranayama* (breathing exercise) that one controls their vital air. We now know that breathing patterns are affected by mood, and some people think that breathing in a particular way can itself affect mood. For example, taking a deep breath helps one feel relaxed. People who follow Oxycise claim that breathing increases oxygen that is used in metabolism. By proper breathing, we can increase the oxygen in our body and thus increase metabolism. Increased metabolism, according to followers of oxycise, can help in losing weight. One thing we can be sure of is that right breathing is important in controlling one's mood and staying healthy. No wonder even my watch reminds me to breathe time and again. One who is in control of his/her mind is in the third stage called *manomaya,* when he/she figures out the values of life. Individuals controlled by *manomaya* or mind seek the company of family, friends, or any kind of groups. The huge chunk of middle class falls into this category, where the basic survival needs are fulfilled. Those who cannot control the mind would not be able to control his or her reaction to adverse situations. This can lead to build up of stress and depression. It is through the fifth limb of yoga called *pratyahara* that one controls the mind. *Pratyahara* means drawing back or retreat, not necessarily physically. With practice, one can block the signals coming from the sense organs from consciously registering in your mind. It prepares a person to be unaffected by outside events and be in full emotional control. At this stage, one can take care of one's sense of belonging. It is believed that loneliness and depression will not affect such a person even at trying times. The next stage is *vijnanamaya,* a stage when one desires status, power, respect and self-esteem. It is through *dhyana* or meditation that one controls one's intellect. Through *dhyana*, one loses the need for self-esteem. Pride and ego cease to exist and you become aware of how you are thinking. You become cognizant about your biases through introspection. You can evaluate your deepest thoughts, feelings and all the information coming through your senses in a dispassionate manner. This final stage of spiritual bliss is known as the *anandamaya*. It is achieved when one manages to control the casual body. This is the point where one reaches the state of self-actualization and gains the ability to have a thoughtless state of mind for a substantial amount of time. If one can control that state, one can be happy whenever one wants, because the brain is now trained to secrete the right neurotransmitters at will, without need of an external stimuli.

Who are we?

'Who are we?' is a question we have been asking ourselves for thousands of years. Unfortunately, we don't yet have a good answer. Some would say that we are what we are made of, like the atoms. That makes us eternal as long as the universe exists. Replicators evolved from atoms. These genetic codes had developed their own identity. Hence, some individuals might say that we are what makes us, i.e. the genes. The genes evolved and crafted conscious brains that created a new identity through information. Maybe we are just that information created by our memories. That makes us eternal as long as the memory can be stored. None of these definitions gives us a unique identity, separate from the rest of the universe. Our form is a cyclic process made from a collection of small atoms. There is no uniqueness there. Our code is a collection of many genes that change over time. You cannot find a unique 'us' in the genes. The information itself is collection of many moments that can be split or mixed, without the need of having uniqueness. May be there is no satisfying answer because the question itself stems from our ego of giving meaning to our otherwise meaningless life.

There is a prevalent thought that the true us is our soul. Most religious schools have their own version of soul. They claim that Near Death Experiences (NDE) and Out of Body Experiences (OBE) have proven its existence. This claim, unfortunately, is not true. Our faith in soul is like the seven colours of the rainbow. We learn about it from our childhood and the belief in soul is deeply rooted in our sub-conscious mind. Soul gives us the hope that we are something rather than nothing. The claims of NDE and OBE have both been explained by science. Just where the spinal cord meets the posterior part of the brain lies our brainstem. Brainstem has been proven to function independently of the higher brain. This fascinating part of the brain triggers Rapid Eye Movement (REM) intrusion, or in simple words hallucinations or dreaming while still being awake. So, even when other parts of the brain are dead, brainstem continues to function. Our brainstem gives the feeling of passing through tunnels, or meeting dead relatives, and even god while nearly dead. OBEs are more interesting. In such cases, you actually feel like you are outside the body. Your perception about space and your body's relative position gets mixed up. There is a region in the parietal lobe of the brain called angular gyrus that is involved with spatial recognition. It makes us aware of our body and its situation in space. Experiments have proved that when this part of the brain is electrically stimulated, it triggers OBEs.

In Chapter 2 we have seen how our brain makes sense of space, and how the reality that it weaves is just stories. The stories are so strong that it becomes a hard reality for us. The apparent feeling of being out of the body and sensing the surrounding in details, is part of that story. Once experienced, there is no way of recognizing what's real and what's not. I must add that none of the scientific experiments nullifies the possibility of existence of soul or spiritual experiences. However, the claim of soul being proven is still a fantasy. Else, someone would have received a Nobel Prize for it. At this moment, I do not have any convincing reason to believe in the popular story that we are nothing but our souls.

On the contrary, there is enough evidence about the thing that makes us. A collection of atoms makes our cells, a collection of cells makes us, collection of us makes matter, and a collection of matter makes the universe. We all are performing our jobs with a sense of separation from each other, just like the individual cells at their own level. Is their conscience and sense of separation at each scale? Our nature of giving meaning to everything created the desire to answer the question 'who are we?' The more one tries to answer it, the more one realize the insignificance of our tiny selves. The question shifts from 'who are we?' to 'why are we?' No one knows the answer to that question. Maybe we just are. Within our limited existence, self-actualization seems to be very important to most of us.

Maslow studied the characters for few famous personalities, who, he believed, had attained self-actualization, like, Abraham Lincoln, Thomas Jefferson, and Albert Einstein. Twelve important characteristics of such persons, as noted by Maslow, are:

1. They are not molded by cultures, but by their own free thinking.
2. They accept themselves as they are, including the positives and negatives.
3. They enjoy the journey as much as the destination.
4. Despite being unconventional, they do not want to shock or disturb.
5. They embrace the unknown and the ambiguous.
6. They are humble.
7. They are grateful.
8. They have deep relation with few people, but are affectionate towards the entire human race.
9. They are motivated by growth.
10. They have a purpose in life.
11. They look at the bigger picture, and not bothered by 'small things'.
12. Despite all this, they are not perfect.

The whole process of achieving self-actualization is simply about controlling one's body by staying fit, controlling one's mind by meditation, and after self-introspection and enough knowledge, one gets into the state of *intachment*. Thus, one is involved with everything, but gets affected by nothing. The other way of looking at it is that you train your brain to secrete the right neurotransmitters according to your want, rather than that of the situation you are in. This means, you control your mind, and not the other way round. One must not forget that our mind is a complex organ, and there is no simple workflow to achieve self-actualization. These methods are guides, and no sharp boundary exists between the categories. A person's mood and behaviour can change with time and situation. If blind faith works for you, so be it. If craziness works for you, fine. Maybe you are the sincere hardworking type. Go for it. There is no one rule that works for all. We need to understand that diversity and respect each other's path. Once one achieves self-actualization, it does not mean the task is done. Keeping one in the state of eternal bliss is a continuous process of keeping one's mind trained. It is like keeping your body fit by regular exercise. You cannot work out in the gym once, and become free to relish pizza and beer for the rest of your life without worry. Though you wish that was true. Being happy is not a one-time effort, but a lifestyle choice. How do you make that choice?

Question 5

How To Be Happy?

'We do not become satisfied by leading a peaceful and prosperous existence. Rather, we become satisfied when reality matches our expectations. The bad news is that as conditions improve, expectations balloon.'

– Yuval Noah Harari, *Homo Deus: A Brief History of Tomorrow* (2018)

The magic wand

Kolkata, a city stuck in time, is often called the City of Joy. The busy streets, the hand-pulled rickshaws, dented and painted public buses, the damp houses, faint Rabindra Sangeet from far away, and the smell of coffee – Kolkata still holds on to her lazy charm. On the side of one such busy street is a small white house where a miracle just happened. At the corner of a dimly lit room sat a saint, with a long white beard, a red tilak on his forehead, dressed in saffron robes. He touched the head of a cancer patient few months ago. Today, the elated patient is here, rolling at the feet of the sadhu baba, because today he was a patient no more. His cancer has miraculously healed. Miracles are performed all over the globe and are taken as the sign of the presence of the divine. Faith trumps over logic... but statistics trumps over faith. According to a study, one out of 60,000 patients recovers from cancer without any medical explanation. The statistics of faith healing from around the globe is no different from the statistics of all cancer patients. Such miracles are more of a proof of how less we know about disease and its cure, than of divine power. Magic healings has been practiced since times immemorial. Most tribal cultures consider pain as influence of evil. Various evil purging rituals, like dancing, singing, yoga, tantra, and even magic spells have been proven effective in healing pain. In the month of October, over forty thousand devotees, many of whom are suffering from pain, visit El Sorte Mountain in Venezuela, the spiritual centre of the cult of Maria Lionza. Various healing rituals are performed during this holy month that are supposed to drive evil spirits away. It is the bad spirits that they consider as cause of pain, and once they are gone, people are happy again. Such ancient customs are not just restricted to ancient villages. Our modern cities also have similar tools that are sold online and claim to provide instant pain relief. There are zero point magical wands sold in Singapore that will relieve your pain like a Harry Porter wand. All you need to do is to wave it round and round the area where it is paining. This method is called the zero point as it 'claims' to re-connect your cells with universal energy, whatever that energy is. Then there are magical oils and even magic lasers that can heal your pain. Faith healing works as long as people have faith. And because it works, like placebo medicines, it is so popular around the globe. At times, faith can work even better than medicines in dragging a person out of disease, trauma, depression and pain.

Pain is unpleasant, yet very important. Without physical pain, we would have never bothered to heal our wounds, and would have easily succumbed to injuries and infection. Without mental pain, you would have happily done things that would have decreased your chance of survival. Pain can at times continue long after the wound has healed. This is called pain memory, and it proves that pain exists in our brain. The good news is, the brain has the power to erase it too. Pain is not something that cannot be controlled if the reward is great. Opioids are pain erasers that attach itself to the receptors of the brain and block pain. This calming and anti-depressing effect is called the 'opioid effect' which our body uses at times of emergency. Sometimes, winning over pain to get rid of it is in itself a great reward. It is through endurance of pain that greatness is achieved. And for some tribes, it is through endurance of pain that you become an adult.

The Okipa ceremony of Mandan Indians is the celebration of earth's creation and warriors prove their courage during the festival by surviving intense pain. The warriors, those who proudly take part in the competition, are starved, have their skin slit, hanged, and their endurance is rewarded by chopping off their pinkie finger. That is just the beginning. Those who survive need to run their last run where they have to perform life-threatening stunts. If you manage to get out alive and complete the run, you will gain respect and fame. You will be declared an adult. The winners are all set to become the next leaders. It may sound horrible and painful, but that's the price you pay to prove your worth. Some warriors proudly claim to have done it twice, though I am not sure which finger they cut off next.

Pain and stress can have quite an effect in our lives. Our body releases cortisol hormone during stress, which reduces our immunity against disease. It has the potential to even alter our genes. A study done on a NASA astronaut named Scott Kelly, who had stayed for an entire year in space, showed how stress of staying in space has altered his genes. Even after two years of his return from space, 7% of his genetic expressions due to stress in space did not return to baseline. The baseline was drawn by comparing with his identical twin brother.

Studies have also shown that pre-natal exposure to stress affects the behaviour of children in their adult life. Such stressed children seem to have early onset of puberty, probably because the body thinks that its chances of surviving for long is bleak. What is more important is that such change does not last just for one generation. The information of stress gets written into the genes and can be propagated down the generations through epigenetic inheritance. Stressed children grow up to become stressed parents, who in turn give birth to stressed children. Stress is one of the biggest killers of modern society. It can lead to digestive disorder, insomnia, depression, sexual dysfunction and obesity. Stress also causes heart related diseases and is so severe in Japan, China and South Korea that they even have a name for it. In Japan, it is called *karoshi*, in China as *guoloasi*, and in South Korea as *gwarosa*. The literal translation of these words is 'overwork death', and includes heart attack and stroke due to stress and starvation diet. Pain and stress are subjective and every person has their own level of tolerance, depending on genes, emotions and environments. While drugs like opium poppy can heal pain just like natural opioids, they might have unwanted side effects. Luckily, there is a simple way to reduce stress. It has been demonstrated by Sheldon Cohen in an experiment that individuals who slept more than seven hours daily had less stress and better immunity. If you have work overload, go for a siesta. You can now even justify a power nap to your manager. There is another way of not getting affected by stress. Studies have shown that subjects who believed that stress affects health negatively were found to be more affected by it then those who did not believe in the same. Ignorance, at times, can be bliss.

There are times when it seems like there is no way out of misery. Life becomes too depressing. 2018 World Health Organization report reveals that India is leading the list of most depressed countries in the world, followed by China and USA. These are absolute numbers, and the top countries also are the most populous ones. But the problem is still significant, and luckily most of the time there is a way out of depression. That path may be a difficult one. Childhood trauma or suffering a great loss can cause depression. This can lead to emotional suffering and mental agony leading to social isolation. A recent Cell paper by Zelikowsky et al. (2018) found that social isolations for long periods of time reshape the chemistry of the brain. The experiments showed that socially isolated mouse had high level of stress with the increase in the brain signaling molecule Tac2. This in turn increased the level of neuropeptide called NkB. You might not like it, but your brain has similar pathways to that of the mice. It is highly likely that we are affected in the same way. NkB affects specific regions of the brain, and the signs of stress include anxiety and aggression. The study further showed that intake of drugs that inhibit Tac2 and NkB resulted in reduction of stress. This proves that use of medication and psychotherapy can help recover people who are suffering from post-traumatic stress disorders (PTSD). Even people with borderline personality disorder (BPD), caused by genetic, brain, environmental, and social factors, can be cured by changing the chemistry of the brain. Since depression is just biochemistry of the brain, shock therapy and faith can work like a magic wand. But, can faith go wrong?

Eggs of faith

Greylag goose is a large species of goose that has mottled and barred grey and white plumage along with orange beaks and pink legs. These cute romantic creatures generally pair for life. The geese lay their eggs in the ground behind shrubs or bushes and the eggs can get easily displaced. A Greylag goose brings back her displaced egg into the nest easily by rolling it with her beak and neck without damaging it. This is an inherent talent built in their genes, and they are so obsessed with this behaviour that even if you keep any other spherical object nearby, she would roll it back into her nest. She just cannot help it. Human beings too have our eggs of faith. When someone puts some information in front of us, no matter how fake it is, if it fits our faith, we are going to roll it back into our nest. We just cannot help it. It is normal human tendency to only verify information that does not fit our prejudice. When it perfectly fits the bill, we tend not to check the facts. That's when we tend to believe a lie. And when a lie is repeated over and over again, it becomes a truth.

A majority of Americans think that 33% of their population are immigrants. The real number is just 14%. Many Indians believe that the Muslim population in India is over 30%. The true reported number is only 14.2%. Ignorance gives rise to conspiracy theories. And therein lies the problem. Ignorance isn't always bliss. 'Post-truth' is Oxford dictionary's word of the year for 2016. It is an adjective meaning, 'Relating to or denoting circumstances in which objective facts are less influential in shaping public opinion than appeals to emotion and personal belief'. Politicians funded news channels, rise of social media and internet, insecurity resulting from the declining economy and rising terrorism and polarization of political ideologies are few of the many reasons for the birth of the post-truth era. Post-truth politics is said to have played its role in the Brexit referendum and US presidential election. Our mind is wired in a way that it is easy to fall for misinformation.

Misinformation is used to trigger riots and wars. Misinformation feeds racism and creates an industry like 'fair and lovely' out of it. Misinformation creates intolerance, ISIS being a live example of that. But ISIS is not the only example. Marshal Khan was tortured, shot at, and even after he died, his dead body was beaten to a pulp by his fellow students in Abdul Wali Khan University. His guilt? He was secular and liberal and thus, according to the murderous mob, blasphemous. Twenty-eight-year-old Nazimuddin Samad, an atheist blogger, was hacked to death in Bangladesh because he wrote what he felt was right. Srinivas Kuchibhotla, a thirty-year-old Indian, was shot in Kansas USA because he was a non-American working in America. Pehlu Khan, a fifty-five-year-old man from Haryana was murdered by '*gau-rakshaks*' (cow protectors) in Rajasthan just because the mob suspected him and his friends of illegally transporting cows. Ignorance has taken more lives than any weapon in history of human civilization, how can it be bliss? Ignorance not just creates stress in a person's life, but also creates stress for the society as a whole. This in turn reduces the happiness index of the society. In order to build a happy society, we need to have an education system that teaches children how to handle information. In this era of the internet and overload of information, it is essential to have the skill set to distinguish truth from fake.

Is it possible to get rid of ignorance completely? The capacity of our human brain is limited. Large Hadron Collider can churn out thirty times more data in a year than the total storage capacity of our brain. There is only so much we can store. In this age of information, we need to depend on the knowledge of others to believe in something. Neither do we have money and time, nor the skills required to verify each and every piece of information that comes our way. If you question everything, then you have nothing to begin with. We believe in evolution, plate tectonics and the Big Bang because we believe in the word of someone or some journal we trust. These are not even facts, but theories that most of us have never personally tested in detail. When an orthodox Christian says that evolution is fake because he/she believes in the word of someone else who she/he trusts, how do we say that he/she is wrong? Yes, there are reasons. But the reasons do not matter from the perspective of a believer. Thousands of years ago, some pretty reliable persons said that the earth was flat. We 'saw' it and believed it. But they were wrong. Newton, a pretty reliable physicist in my opinion, told us how gravity works and we believed him. But he was wrong. It is never an easy thing to separate facts from fiction. There will always be things we can never verify. It is a slippery ground. But that does not mean you will let others exploit your ignorance. Luckily, there are few things you can do to prevent yourself from getting fooled. Question the authenticity of the source, especially before you plan to share information with others and potentially spread a lie (very well knowing that even a reliable source like Newton can be wrong). Never believe someone who tells you to have blind faith. Any person who does not want you to ask tough questions, is a person who does not have enough knowledge to answer the questions. The next thing would be to question the motive behind the information you received. Is it trying to spread hatred? Does it have an ulterior motive? Check your eggs before rolling them into your nest. The trick is to have an open mind and challenge the prejudice. Ask yourself if you believe in something just because you were told by people close to you, or you actually spent some time thinking about it. Ignorance is bliss only if you know you are ignorant.

In pursuit of happiness

Search the internet and you will find thousands of ways of how to be happy – from buying a cat to donating an organ. Obviously happiness is something that is damn important to all of us. In no other era in the history of mankind did we have so many reasons to be happy than the one we are living in. Recent statistics, including the one by Steven Pinker, show that violence is at an all-time low. There is a dramatic reduction in war deaths, domestic violence, racism and murder globally. While we have scanty data for the ancient world, we can say that these numbers are certainly true for the last few centuries. World energy consumption, an indicator of our lifestyle, is also increasing exponentially. Energy consumption increased six times since 1960, while the population grew just 2.2 times. The middle class now has more luxury than any medieval king could have dreamt of. With all the reasons we have to be happy, are we any happier?

While there is a direct correlation between GDP and per capita energy consumption, the relation between Human Development Index (HDI) and per capita energy consumption is a bit tricky. HDI is calculated from various factors, including life expectancy at birth, years of schooling, and per capita gross national income. It is often used as a proxy for happiness. Overall, the HDI gets better with per capita energy consumption. However, there is a lot of scatter at the lower energy consumption area, and above a particular amount of energy consumption, it does not improve the HDI (Figure 6). Surveys done over time in developed countries have shown that, despite increase in income, people are not getting happier. Once the basic physiological (*annamaya*) needs are fulfilled, money doesn't really make you happy. People are in fact getting lonelier and depressed. As a result, suicide rates are increasing at an alarming pace. Self-harm is the leading cause of death in today's world. India has one of the highest suicide rates in the world and it is going to get worse unless something is done. Despite the luxuries, why is happiness eluding us?

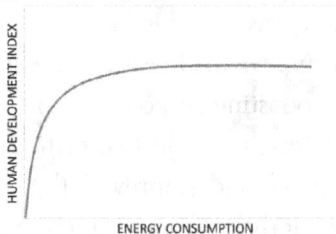

Figure 6: Schematic Plot showing that happiness increases with development only till the basic needs are fulfilled. After that, increase in energy consumption does not increase happiness.

In her paper 'Money Giveth, Money Taketh Away – The Dual Effect of Wealth on Happiness' published in 2010, Quoidbach et al. demonstrates that 'having access to the best things in life may actually undercut people's ability to reap enjoyment from life's small pleasures'. She came to that conclusion after two different experiments. In the first experiment she found out that wealthy people savoured chocolates less than the less wealthy ones. In the second experiment, one set of people were primed by showing them pictures of money, while the other was not. Despite similar economic background, those who saw pictures of money before tasting chocolates, savoured the chocolates less than those who were not shown pictures of money. The sheer thought of money increase the expectation levels. If peace, money, or lifestyle is not making people happy, then what will? A bacteria maybe!

A particular type of bacteria in the soil in your backyard can actually make you happy (read: get you high). Does that surprise you? A creature so small that you cannot see can actually control the way you behave! The culprit here is a bacterium named *Mycobacteriumvaccae*. This was discovered quite accidentally in 2004 by an oncologist at the Royal Marsden Hospital named Mary O'Brien. She was injecting lung cancer patient with serum from *Mycobacteriumvaccae* because the bacterium was thought to have immune boosting response on patients. While the test failed to fulfil its original objective of healing cancer, it made the patients happier and improved their lifestyle. After the surprising results of the test, more studies were done and it was proven that bacteria and bacterial products can have effects on the brain and the neural pathways in a way that it affects human behaviour. Bacteria can even order you what to eat. If your tummy is full of carbohydrate loving bacteria, that's what it will make you order. The exact process of how it manages to do that is not clear. Bacteria communicates using neurotransmitters, which also controls our emotions. That is how our emotions work. It is controlled not by the external situation you are in, but by your internal biochemistry. Chemicals inside you affect your emotions, external factors can only activate those chemicals.

Nicole Lazzaro explains that there are four different chemicals released by the brain (neurotransmitters) that can make you happy – dopamine, oxytocin, serotonin and endorphins. Each type of happiness due to the different neurotransmitters is dissimilar. Dopamine is released on anticipation of a happy event or stress. It controls human emotions, including desires, achievements, pleasures, mood, sleep and happiness. Oxytocin, also known as the 'love hormone', is released by the pituitary gland, especially when one comes in close proximity to another person. It sometimes has the effect of 'falling in love' and is also called the 'cuddle hormone'. It helps in relationships and bonding and the resulting feeling of happiness caused by oxytocin secretion is different from the happiness due to pleasure or achievement created by dopamine. Serotonin's effect on happiness is debatable, however, it has been proven that this hormone helps in learning. Some people claim that it affects the mood, and lack of it can make one feel low. Endorphins are known to mask pain and discomfort. They can be released during vigorous exercise and lead to an effect termed as 'runners' high'. Again, the happiness from endorphins is different from the other three. There must be several other chemicals that affect our mood than the four described by Lazzaro. The secretion of these chemicals may or may not be caused by external situations. It can be artificially triggered by drugs or meditation. And, more importantly, it does not depend on the amount of energy you consume, or how luxurious a life you live. Instead, it depends on your expectations, rather the deviation of what you get from what you expected. When a person gets richer, his or her desires and expectations also rise. Soon the difference between expectations and happiness reaches base level and your happiness decreases. Psychologists call it 'hedonic treadmill' effect. The lower the expectations are, the happier that person is. That is why religions like Buddhism asks you to renounce materialistic pleasure to get out of the cycle of suffering. By renouncing all your wants, you bring your expectations to the lowest possible base level. There is only one way your happiness go from there. But, it that the only way to be happy?

Happiness is a result of trial and error of millions of years of evolution. Couple of years ago, professors Meike Bartels and Philipp Koellinge have found the genes that might be responsible for happiness, after studying DNA samples from 298,000 people from around the globe. They found that the prevalence of the FAAH gene, which makes a protein that affects feelings of pleasure and pain, correlates fairly well with 'happiness' of different countries. If evolution indeed favoured happiness, the question is why? We are not going to survive for long if we are equally happy to see our enemies as we are when we see our friends. According to evolutionary psychologist Robert Cummins of Deakin University of Melbourne, happiness evolved because it gave us adaptive advantage. It is same for the negative emotions of fear, anger and disgust. Negative emotions are stronger because they are more critical. Even though most snakes are clinically non-venomous, when we see a snake, we throw the statistics out of the window and run. Fear helps us run away from the predator, anger helps us beat our opponents and disgust helps us avoid poisonous food. Experiments done by psychologists Daniel Kahneman and Amos Tversky demonstrated that 'pain is more urgent than pleasure'. That is the reason, despite reasons to be happy, we always come back to the base level of happiness. Evolution made sure that we do not become complacent and get killed. Once we are safe, however, happiness increases our want to survive. Fredrickson's 'broaden and build' theory proposes that happiness helps us build resources and store for the future. If we were not happy eaters, we would have starved to death; if we were not happy 'maters', we would have gone extinct long ago. Positive feelings like happiness change the way our brains work and helps us gather more information. Studies have shown that happy people are also healthier. While small wonders like a child's smile, pleasant weather, a bird's song, the green forest, the blue sky, food, beer and sex can make us happy, we somehow end up confusing ourselves asking the question, 'what makes us happy?' A better question to ask yourself will probably be, 'Am I happy?' If the 4.5 billion years of earth history was compressed in a single day, our civilization would only last a few seconds, and 'your' life in that? Insignificant! If the whole universe were this room, your galaxy would be smaller than an atom, and you in that? Insignificant! When you realize how insignificant the perceived you is, you realize that your life is a joke. The trick is to laugh at it. Let's be happy in that insignificant instant when we are just 'us'. The next section will help you plan just that.

The Excel of life

F|ew days back, I was playing with the miracle software called MS Excel and ended up creating something that shocked me. It made me look at my life from an entirely different perspective. All I made was a 45-row by 24-column matrix (Figure 7). Each column in that Excel sheet represents a month and each row a year. Every year has 12 months and the assumption is that you live till 90. Two years (24 months) have been stacked in one row for convenience. Ideally you should make a 90-row by 12-column matrix. 42-row by 24-column just have a better dimension for my screen. So the 1080 months of our life is now converted to 1080 cells. When I looked at the Excel, I made my first reaction was, boy it is not that big! One month passes at the blink of an eye. All the months that I will ever live fits in just one screen! I realized I don't have much time left. The more I looked at it the more it got worse.

The message is clearly out there – there aren't many boxes left! To realize it, just like I did, create one excel for your life. Colour all the months that you have spent. Fill it with all the happy events of your life, events that has happened or you think might happen. If you have wishes, decide a date and put them there. Now mark all those happy memories in your 'Excel of life' by colouring the cell red. Then check how many red boxes you have and how many you have planned for. The number of red cells there is the actual measure of your happiness. You will be surprised by what you find. This excel will help you make your financial plans as well by telling you how much money you need for achieving the things you want, like your child's education or a world tour. This small excel is a really powerful tool to sort your life.

We are all born with a terminal disease called ageing. We will eventually run out of life. Make the most of it now, when you can. Most of us tend to over plan for the future. We try and save a lot for the future. If your plan is to save now and enjoy after retirement, think again. Even if we ignore old age and disease, how many excel cell will you actually have at that time? Only 65% people live to be 80 years. Believe me, no matter how young you are, your life still comes with an expiry date. That is not necessarily a bad thing. Eternity is boring and possibly dangerous. Your brains can only take in so much information. It will be saturated after a point of time. Your bones will become weak. Cumulative injuries are going to wear away your body. You will lose your teeth, and possibly your hair and eye sight too. There is only one way out of the misery of eternal life. Replace your body and reformat your memory. In many ways, that's exactly what life does with death. The *mememtomori*, meaning 'remember you must die', was once an important icon that reminded people that death is inevitable. Let this excel trigger you to take a little break from seriousness and find time for happiness. Major part of your adult life, you will be 'working' for someone, or yourself, to earn money. We saw earlier that it does not matter how much money you earn, if you earn enough to not be in poverty. Your profession is important, but not more than your life. So, it makes sense to choose the job you like, rather than the one that gives you money or status. Happiness will betray you if you try to live up to other's expectations. Your status, your luxurious house, that red Ferrari, is not worth it if the cost is your entire adult life. Live for yourself. It is time to take control of your life. *Non ducor, duco*.

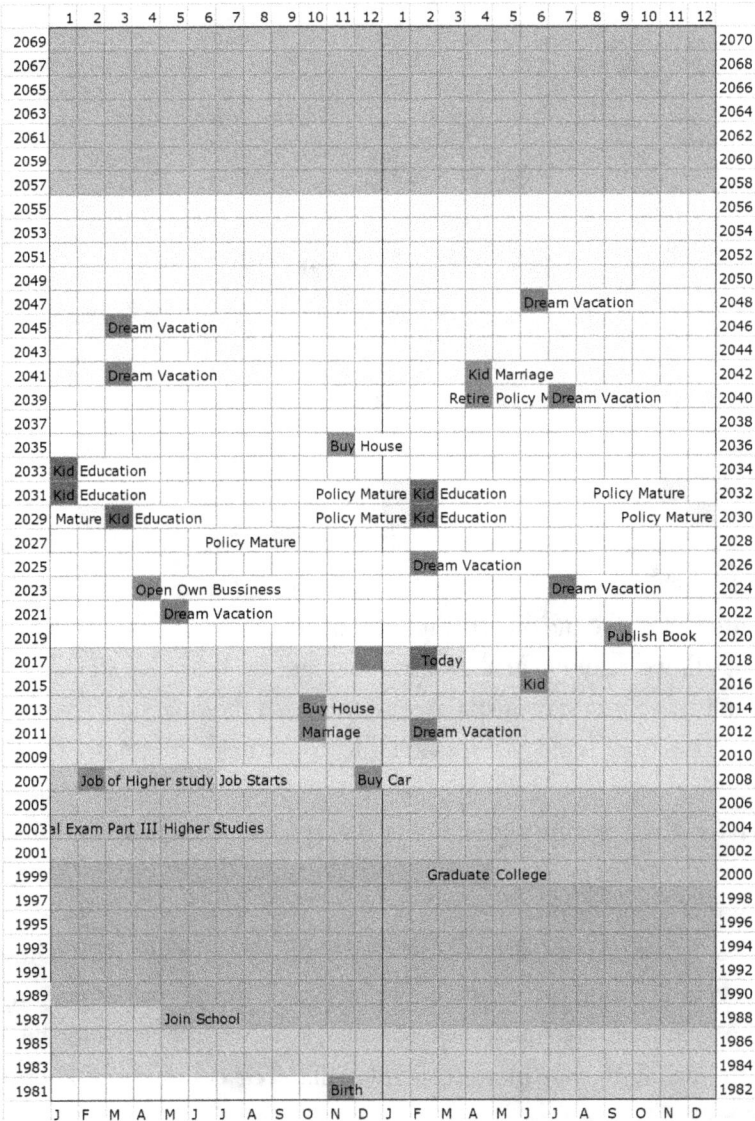

Figure 7: Example of an Excel of Life

How to be happy?

For our known universe, it all started with the Big Bang, which had the right initial conditions to form complicated life forms like the one reading these lines now. Why it happened at all, we may never know. Physics said let there be star dust, and there was star dust. Chemistry turned the dust into organic matter and biology breathed life into these proteins. Then evolution sculpted the apes. Fire, language and agriculture had been the key turning points of our species. Language and the development of symbol-centric brain created god, clans, tribes, borders and civilization. It has made us social animals. The way we 'hallucinate reality', is governed by the stories we learn. Our symbolic-brain helps our community stay together by holding on to a common narrative. There was a time when our ownership to our family was more important than our community. There was a time when our ownership to our king, region, and regional gods was more important than a non-existent nation. Now we live in an era where nation is more significant than community or religion. Maybe in the future, globalization and the common environmental threats will turn us into a single global community. The stories we believe in, the stories of what's important and what's right, change with time. From stones to arrows, from guns to nuclear weapons, civilizations have come a long way. Science and technology began to grow as each clan wanted to out-do the other, each nation wanting to be the super power. The primitive urge of survival is still the dominant instinct in all *Homo sapiens*. But our problems changed with time. No more do we need to worry about how to hunt down the next meal. No more do we need to worry about famines. Instead of missed hunt, we now worry about missed meetings. Instead of worrying about how to fight to be the tribe leader, we worry about promotion. While the cause of stress has changed, the biology of stress remains the same.

Resting in an infinitesimally small corner of the universe, for an infinitesimally small amount of time, these insignificant 'brain with little brawn' apes have asked a very significant question, 'Why?' Science has been able to answer a lot of 'what', 'when', 'where', 'who' and 'how'. Science may tell you that there are six 'flavours' of quarks, three 'generations' of neutrinos, and one Higgs particle. But why so? Why do the 19 universal constants have that particular value which leads to life? Why are we here, why was there a Big Bang, or why anything exists at all? Maybe the 'why' has no meaning because all possible universes exist and we are in the one with the specific conditions that favours us. In our mission to answer the 'why', we have got other revelations. We have realized that we are nothing different from what the rest of the universe is made of. Since everything in the universe is governed by the laws of physics, it is unlikely that we are not. May be it is physics that wants us to be happy.

Happiness researcher and psychologist Shawn Achor articulates, '90 percent of your long-term happiness is predicted not by the external world, but by the way our brain processes the world.' Recent scientific breakthroughs are constantly reminding us that our perception about us, and the way we behave, is controlled by our bio-chemistry. That biochemistry makes us interpret the same thing in different ways. Maybe the ancient Indians understood this and claimed that the world is *'maya'*. There are more than one truth and there is always a valid alternate perspective. I hope that the reader now appreciates that. The world would become a much happier place once we have the patience to appreciate other perspectives. It is possible to get rid of a lot of our ignorance, stress and pain, provided we are ready to understand what they really are. Unlearning our deep-rooted faith is the most difficult thing to do. But we can train our brain to overcome that challenge. We all have our own way of doing that, depending on our character. Remember how insignificant we are, and thus how insignificant our problems are.

Finding a purpose in life can give you happiness, but to be happy finding purpose is not necessary. Happiness is just a burst of neurons fired in your brain that are reacting to some biochemicals. We have a short life and there is little time to waste our energy on negative things. Keep your body and mind healthy, have a broader view of life, take important decisions when all three components of your brain are in a stable state, create your own excel of life and practice happiness. Neuroscience experiments by studying brain scans of Tibetian monks have shown that meditation and happiness can alter your brain. By practicing happiness, you can control secretion of 'happy' neurotransmitters, that will alter the neural pathways in your brain and turn you into a happy person. While it may sound odd, practicing happiness works like a charm. Achor found in his research that increase in happiness can lead to, 'a 23 percent reduction in stress, 39 percent improvement in health and 31 percent in productivity'. The most important revelation of his study is that success does not bring happiness. Happiness can improve performance and productivity, driving one towards greater success. Most of us are confused about what makes us happy. We look for acquisition of external reasons since they give us temporary happiness. Our genes are programmed to drag that happiness down to the baseline. Happiness depends on internal chemistry, and thus permanent happiness can be achieved by focusing our thoughts towards ourselves, rather than outside ourselves. This is the secret of all ancient philosophies. It is not about finding god, it is not about connecting with your soul; it is a simple science.

Science was born from the want of survival. Science was the fuel that drove the western countries to the top. Science led to industrial revolution, improvement in our living standards, along with the increase in carbon dioxide emission and the resulting global warming threat. We might have just started the sixth great extinction. Our existence, or that of the living world does not matter to the universe. The universe will survive without us, the world will survive without us. Survival of all species and the balance of the natural world matters to us. Because if the balance is broken, we won't survive. Maybe we will create a new balance by moving to another planet. Science has created artificial intelligence that is often seen as a threat. We are trying to bring back extinct animals. That too is seen as a moral degradation by many. On the other hand, we are also trying our luck with eternity, saving memories, replacing temporary body parts with eternal robots, and recreating life itself. Algorithms are slowly taking over our lives. Big data and artificial intelligence can already predict our likes and dislikes, and recommend what we want to buy or where we want to travel. The wearables are constantly monitoring our health, reminding us to walk, stand, and even breathe. The new apple watch can monitor your EGC. The day is not far when they would create a digital replica of us, because our mind is just a very complex algorithm. Your digital clone will think like you even though it might not be able to feel like you. Without the emotional bias, it will be an upgraded version of you that will take better decisions, and more importantly, will be connected to all other individuals through internet (or its better future alternatives). That might just make you irrelevant. How will that future affect religion, god, nationality, and all other emotional mnemes, and ultimately our happiness? Our future will be different from the present one, but the socio-cultural evolution will continue. Maybe technology will someday erase the barriers of religion, caste, creed, race, sex, nationality, or any other sense of separation. Once the boundaries are erased, we might evolve into a single happy interconnected super-organism.

Abraham Lincoln rightly said, 'Most folks are about as happy as they make up their minds to be'. Happiness is not about being happy all the time. It is about being the person one wants to be. It is about the ability to be wrong, it is also about the ability to cry, it is also about being imperfect. Nowadays it has become a fashion to be perfect, strong and happy. Perfection kills creativity. Human beings are made up of a spectrum of emotions. These emotions exist because of a reason. Only when we allow people to be who they are, with all their weaknesses, can they leverage that quality to do great things. There is a word amongst the Bantu tribes of South Africa called *'Ubuntu'*. This Nguni Bantu term means 'I am because we are'. They believe in the universal bond of sharing and caring for each other that helps them survive and keeps them happy. Ubuntu can also be translated as humanity. It was human beings who created words like humanity, equality, secularism, liberty and peace. These words do not exist beyond the human world. They are fictions that we have invented. Even the questions I have dealt with in this book are a construct of our inquisitive mind. In fact, there is probably no objective reality, and everything is just a mere perception. It is our mind that turns random patterns of acoustic waves into music. It creates literature out of lines and curves drawn on a page. It turns basic desire into love. These are powerful inventions. Yes, some of them may be evolutionary, and in our genes, but they are also cultural mnemes. We should be proud of these stories that we have woven. Just like pheromones controls ants' behaviour, mnemes controls the behaviour of humans. If one is fed stories of selfishness, one becomes selfish. If one is fed stories of altruism, one becomes an altruist. Mnemes play a very important part in our society. These stories can be so profound that it can fight against the forces of nature. It can overrule the genetic command and preach abstinence to a priest. While our ancestors killed Neanderthals and giant mammals, they did not know what they were doing. We do not have that excuse. We are facing catastrophic changes, like the sixth extinction, global warming, and even a possible nuclear threat. The only thing that can save us is a new global narrative that can benefit all. We have the power to choose the narrative we want to hold on to – the ones that breed hatred, or the ones that brings peace. The ones that creates separate identities, or the ones that unite. The ones that foster discrimination and bigotry, or the ones that promote love. Together, we have the power to make that choice. It is through these stories that we can create a strong society and a happier world, not just for us, but for all species. That would be the triumph of the inquisitive apes.

Bibliography

Adhikari, S. (2016). *The Journey of Survivors: 70,000-year history of Indian Subcontinent.* Partridge Publishing.

Andrews, K. (2015). *The Animal Mind: An introduction to the Philosophy of Animal Cognition.* London: Routledge.

Ariely, D. (2010). *Predictably Irrational: The hidden forces that shape our decisions.* New York, NY: HarperCollins Publishers.

Bergner, D. (2014). *What do Women Want? Adventures in the Science of Female Desire.* Canongate Books.

Blackmore, S. J. (2005). *Consciousness: A very Short Introduction. Second revised edition.* Oxford: Oxford University Press.

Brownmiller, S. (1993). *Against Our Will: Men, women and rape.* Ballantine Books.

Bryson, B. (2016). *A Short History of Nearly Everything.* Random House.

Butler, G., & McManus, F. (2014). *Psychology: A Very Short Introduction. Second edition.* Oxford: Oxford University Press.

Close, F.E. (2009). *Nothing: A very short introduction.* Oxford: Oxford University Press.

Covey, S. (1990). *The 7 habits of highly effective people.* Free Press.

Dawkins, R. (1990). *The Selfish Gene. Second edition.* Oxford: Oxford University Press.

Deary, I.J. (2001). *Intelligence: A Very Short Introduction.* Oxford: Oxford University Press.

Diamond, J.M. (1998). *Why is Sex Fun? The Evolution of Human Sexuality.* New York: Basic Books.

Diamond, J.M. (2011). *Collapse: How Societies Choose to Fail or Succeed.* Revised edition. Penguin Books.

Diamond, J.M. (1999). *Guns, Germs, and Steel: The Fates of Human Societies.* New York: W.W. Norton & Company.

Fisher, H.E. (2005). *Why We Love: The Nature and Chemistry of Romantic Love.* Reprint edition. New York: Holt Paperbacks.

Garson, J. (2015). *The Biological Mind: A Philosophical Introduction.* London: Routledge.

Greene, B. (2005). *The Fabric of the Cosmos: Space, Time, and the Texture of Reality.* Reprint edition. Vintage.

Halford, S.G. (2015). *Activate Your Brain: How understanding your brain can improve your work-and your life.* Austin, TX: Greenleaf Book Group Press.

Hammond, C. (2013). *Time Warped: Unlocking the Mysteries of Time Perception.* Edinburgh: Canongate Books.

Harari, Y.N. (2014). *Sapiens: A Brief History of Humankind.* New York: Harper Perennial.

Harari, Y. N. (2017). *Homo Deus: A Brief History of Tomorrow.* New York: Harper Perennial.

Harford, T. (2009). *The Logic of Life: The Rational Economics of an Irrational World.* New York: Random House.

Hawking, S. (1998). *A Brief History of Time.* New York: Bantam Books

Hawking, S.W., &Mlodinow, L. (2012). *The Grand Design. Reprint edition.* New York: Bantam Books.

Heisenberg, W. (2007). *Physics and Philosophy: The Revolution in Modern Science.* Harper Perennial Modern Classics.

Kahneman, D. (2013). *Thinking, Fast and Slow.* Toronto: Anchor Canada.

Krznaric, R. (2013). *How Should We Live? Great Ideas from the Past for Everyday Life.* New York: BlueBridge.

Lane, N. (2016). *The Vital Question: Energy, Evolution, and the Origins of Complex Life.* New York: W.W. Norton & Company.

Lanza, R., Berman, B., & McKnight, A. (2010). *Biocentrism: How Life and Consciousness Are the Keys to Understanding the True Nature of the Universe.* Dallas, Tex: BenBella Books.

Levitt, S.D., & Dubner, S. J. (2010). *Superfreakonomics.* Penguin Books.

Lewis, T., Amini, F., & Lannon, R. (2001). *A general theory of love.* New York: Vintage Books.

Mukherjee, S. (2016). *The Gene: An Intimate History.* Penguin Books Limited.

OShea, M. (2006). *Brain: A Very Short Introduction.* Oxford: Oxford University Press.

Pink, T. (2004). *Free Will: A Very Short Introduction (Very short introductions).* Oxford University Press.

Polkinghorne, J.C. (2002). *Quantum Theory: A Very Short Introduction.* Oxford: Oxford University Press.

Ridley, M. (2010). *Genome: The Autobiography of a Species In 23 Chapters.* New York: MJF Books

Rutherford, A. (2016). *A brief history of everyone who ever lived: The stories in our genes.* London: Weidenfeld& Nicolson.

Ryan, C., &Jethá, C. (2010). *Sex at Dawn: The Prehistoric Origins of Modern Sexuality.* Carlton North, Vic.: Scribe Publications.

Schrodinger, E. (1992). *What is Life?* Cambridge University Press.

Sukel, K. (2012). *Dirty Minds: The Neuroscience of Sex, Love and Relationships.* New York: Free Press.

Wilson, E.O. (1999). *Consilience: The Unity of Knowledge. New edition.* London: Abacus.